YOU CAN DRAW

TRANSFORMERS™

LONDON, NEW YORK, MUNICH,
MELBOURNE, and DELHI

SENIOR DESIGNER Robert Perry
DESIGNER Jon Hall
PUBLISHING MANAGER Simon Beecroft
DTP DESIGNER Hanna Ländin

PROJECT EDITOR Heather Scott
CATEGORY PUBLISHER Alex Allan
PRODUCTION Rochelle Talary
FRONT COVER ART Guido Guidi

First published in the United States in 2007
by DK Publishing
375 Hudson Street, New York, New York 10014

07 08 09 10 11 10 9 8 7 6 5 4 3 2 1
YD022—03/07

Published in Great Britain by Dorling Kindersley Limited

ISBN 978-0-7566-2746-1

A catalog record is available from the Library of Congress.

Color reproduction by Wyndeham Icon Limited, UK
Printed and bound in China by Leo Paper Group

YOU CAN DRAW TRANSFORMERS™

BY SIMON FURMAN

M.Brooks

CONTENTS

INTRODUCTION 6
PENCIL DRAWING 8
EQUIPMENT 10
BASIC SHAPES 12
BASIC FIGURE 14
VARIATIONS 16
VEHICLES 18
PERSPECTIVE 20
BODY PERSPECTIVE 22
TRANSFORMING 24
SHADING & LIGHTING 30
FORESHORTENING 32
ACTION 34
BATTLE! 36
MASTERCLASS: OPTIMUS PRIME 38
HEADS 42
HANDS 44
LEGS & FEET 46
DETAILS 48
WEAPONS 50
GENERATION 1 52
DINOBOTS & INSECTICONS 54
COMBINERS 56
UNICRON 58
BEAST WARS: MAXIMALS 60
BEAST WARS: PREDACONS 62
ARMADA & MINICONS 64
TRANSFORMERS: ENERGON 66
TRANSFORMERS: CYBERTRON 68
STORMBRINGER 70
MASTERCLASS: MEGATRON 72
INKING & COLORING 76
EQUIPMENT 78
INKING EFFECTS 80
COLOR 82
CREATING A COMIC 84
SHOTS & ANGLES 86
SCRIPT & THUMBNAILS 88
FINAL LAYOUT 90
THE END 92
INDEX 94
ACKNOWLEDGMENTS 96

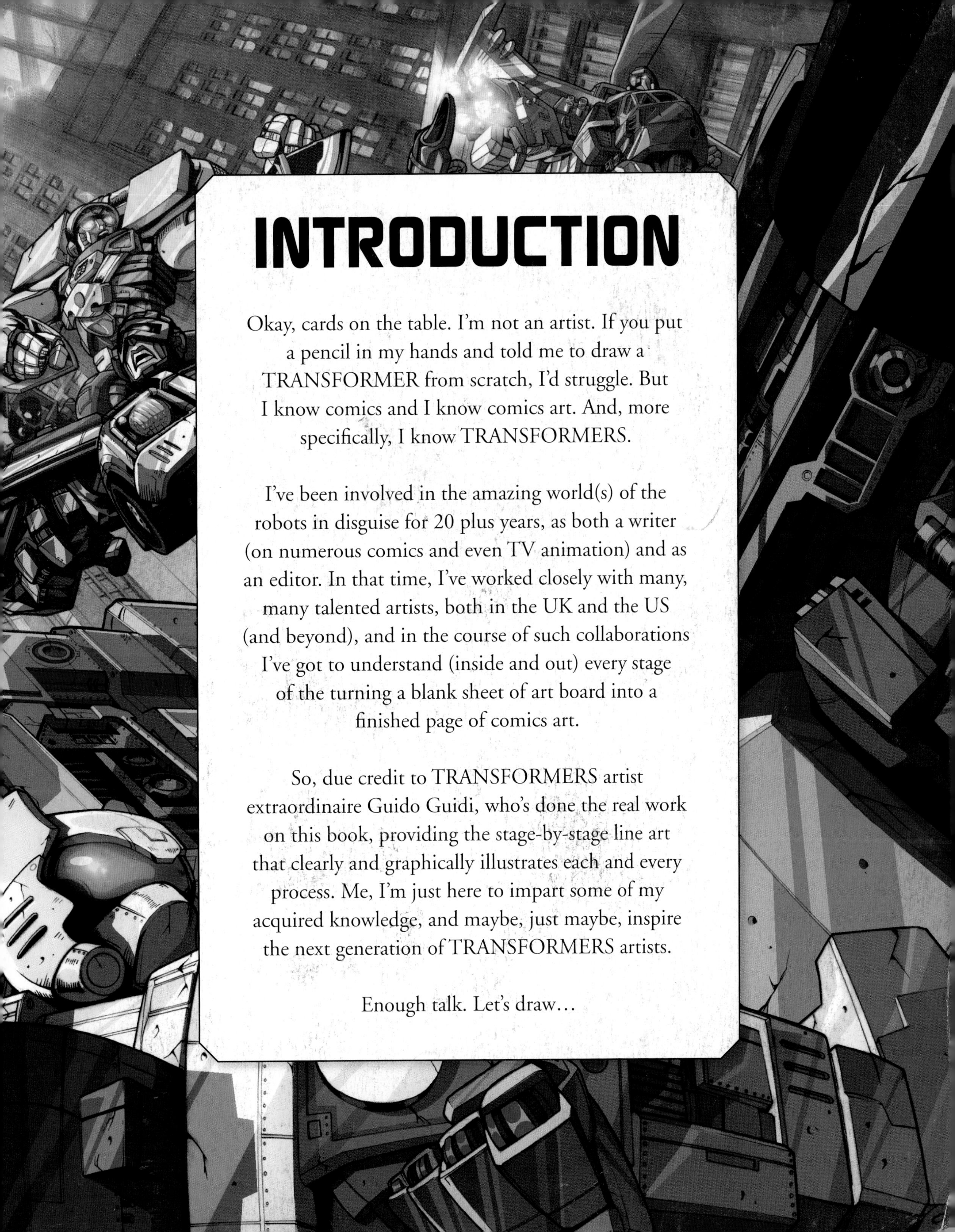

INTRODUCTION

Okay, cards on the table. I'm not an artist. If you put a pencil in my hands and told me to draw a TRANSFORMER from scratch, I'd struggle. But I know comics and I know comics art. And, more specifically, I know TRANSFORMERS.

I've been involved in the amazing world(s) of the robots in disguise for 20 plus years, as both a writer (on numerous comics and even TV animation) and as an editor. In that time, I've worked closely with many, many talented artists, both in the UK and the US (and beyond), and in the course of such collaborations I've got to understand (inside and out) every stage of the turning a blank sheet of art board into a finished page of comics art.

So, due credit to TRANSFORMERS artist extraordinaire Guido Guidi, who's done the real work on this book, providing the stage-by-stage line art that clearly and graphically illustrates each and every process. Me, I'm just here to impart some of my acquired knowledge, and maybe, just maybe, inspire the next generation of TRANSFORMERS artists.

Enough talk. Let's draw...

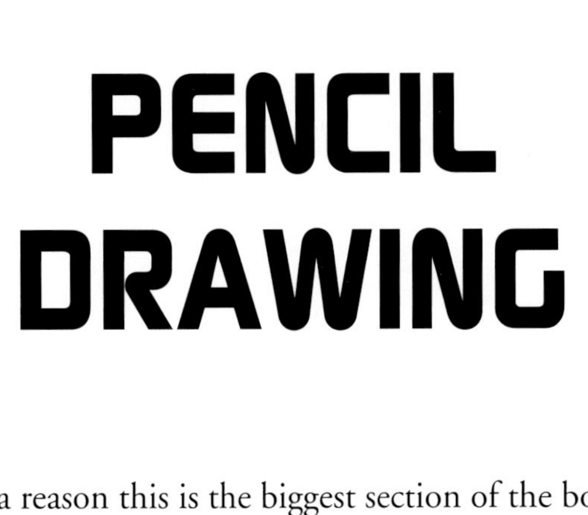

PENCIL DRAWING

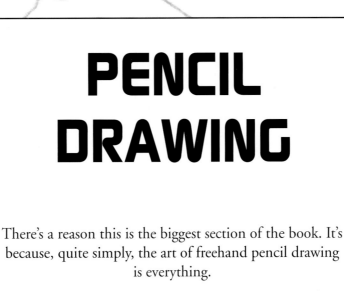

There's a reason this is the biggest section of the book. It's because, quite simply, the art of freehand pencil drawing is everything.

In these days of computer modeling and rendering, of software packages that can ink and color and render, it's easy to forget that the humble pencil is still the most important tool in any artist's armory. Drawing with a pencil, you can do almost anything and go anywhere, all it needs is imagination and the set of skills necessary to apply it properly.

There are no short cuts here. You have to start with the basics and build your penciling skills accordingly, step by step. Over the next 50 or so pages, we'll take you through everything you need, from the essential tools to the construction of figures, scenes, and whole sequential pages, taking in concepts like foreshortening, perspective, and storytelling along the way. And though we're dealing here specifically with TRANSFORMERS, the bulk of these techniques apply across the board.

Pick up your pencil and turn the page. The adventure is about to begin.

EQUIPMENT

PENCILS

The most widely used pencil is an everyday graphite one, but there are other varieties too, such as the mechanical pencil, which holds several thin leads, and the blue pencil, which doesn't show up in photographic reproduction.

Wood-clinched, graphite pencils

Wood-clinched, graphite pencil with eraser

Blue pencil

Mechanical pencil

Lead refills for mechanical pencil

Pencil sharpener

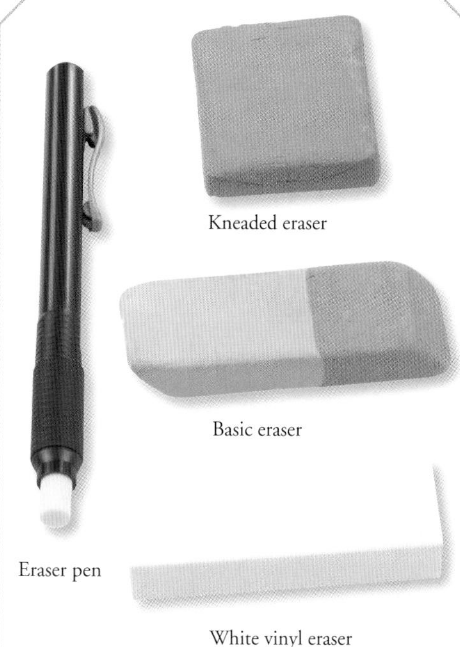

Erasers

Because none of us are perfect, the second most indispensable tool of the artist is the eraser. The white vinyl eraser is gentle and doesn't crumble, which the rubber eraser is prone to do, and the kneaded eraser can be shaped to a specific area of the page. An eraser pen is useful for smaller deletions, as you have more control.

PENCIL MARKS

A different weight of pencil line can be achieved by choosing a different grade of pencil. "H" stands for "hardness" and "B" for "blackness." So, starting from a standard HB pencil, an increased "H" value indicates that the lead is harder, and therefore gives a finer line. With an increased "B" value, the lead gets softer and the line thicker.

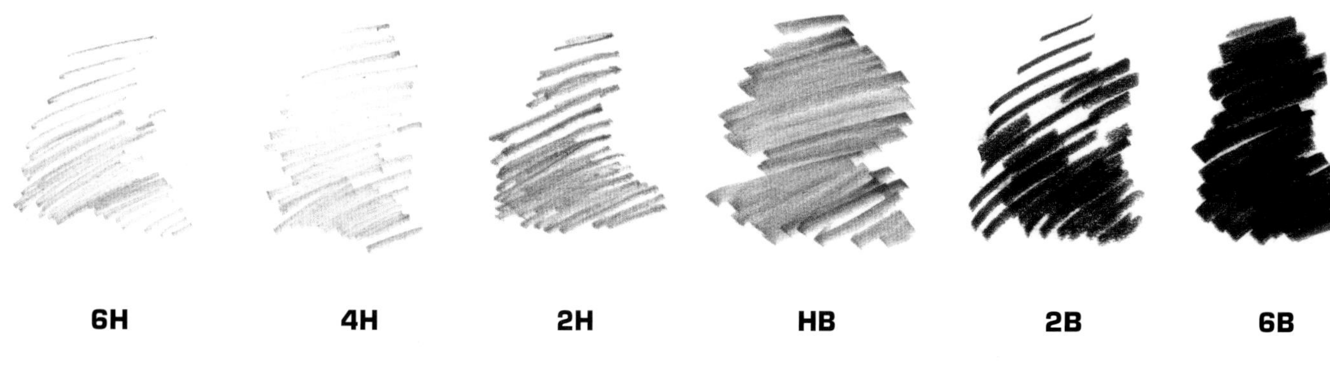

PENCIL GRIP

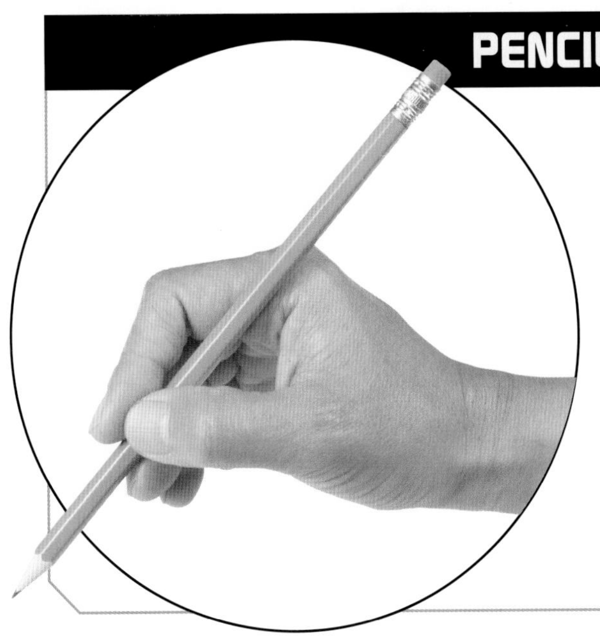

Hold between thumb and middle finger, using the index finger to "steer" the pencil on the page. The grip should be firm but relaxed. Keep your fingers and wrist loose, so as to enable graceful, sweeping lines, and don't press too hard with the point, as this will leave permanent impressions on the page.

TIPS

Use a softer, blunt pencil for the basic sketches. This will stop you adding too many fine details in the early stages, allowing you to focus on the basic shapes and the pose. To lighten up your sketches, use a kneaded eraser, as it won't completely erase your pencils, leaving a ghost image on which you can work. For final penciling, a 0.5mm mechanical pencil is useful for fine details.

Guido Guidi

Other equipment

Always have a ruler or other straight edge to hand, preferably a "raised" ruler, where a portion of the upper plane of the ruler doesn't touch the paper. This slight gap helps prevent smearing. Other useful tools include a triangle or set square, a pair of compasses, assorted stencils, and templates.

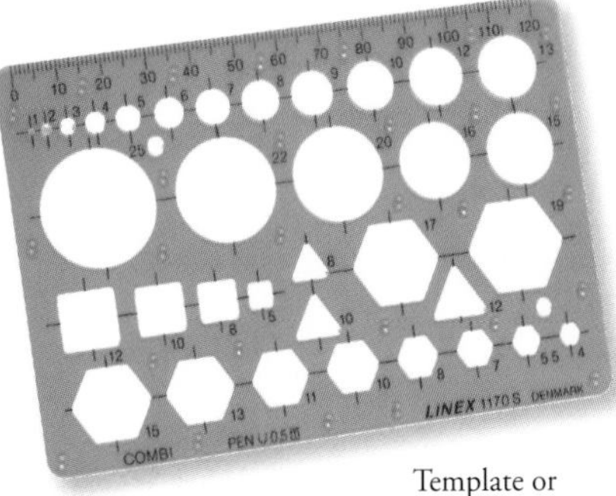

Template or stencil

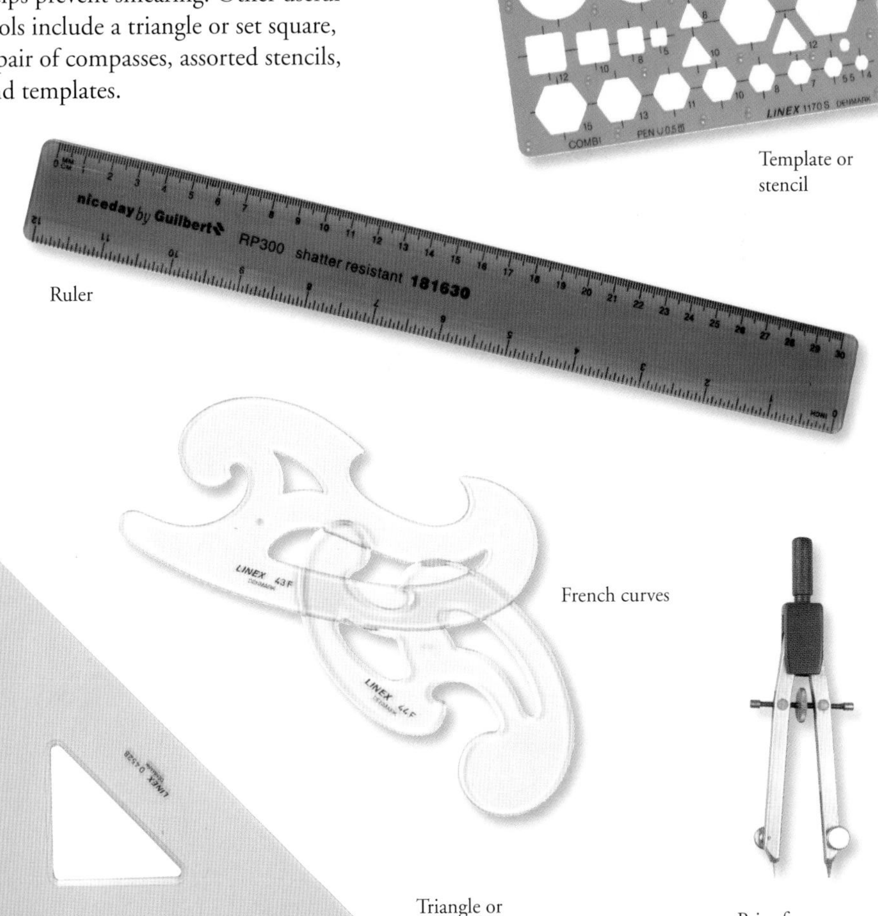

Ruler

French curves

Triangle or set square

Pair of compasses

Rough paper

Smooth paper

Paper

Many professional artists employ bristol board, a durable double-sided art paper intended for longer-term use and preservation. Illustration board is more suitable for artwork that is to be scanned or reproduced on other mediums. Surfaces can be textured or smooth, to preference.

BASIC SHAPES

SHAPING UP

A grasp of basic geometric shapes is essential in most illustrative work, even more so when dealing with robotic beings. There are three main groups. The first includes squares, rectangles, cubes, and cuboids; the second features circles, spheres, and cylinders; and the third consists of triangles and pyramids.

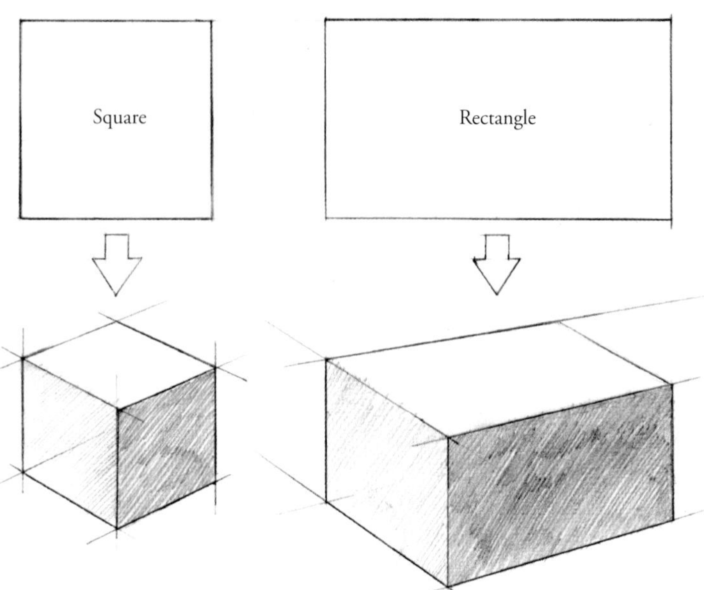

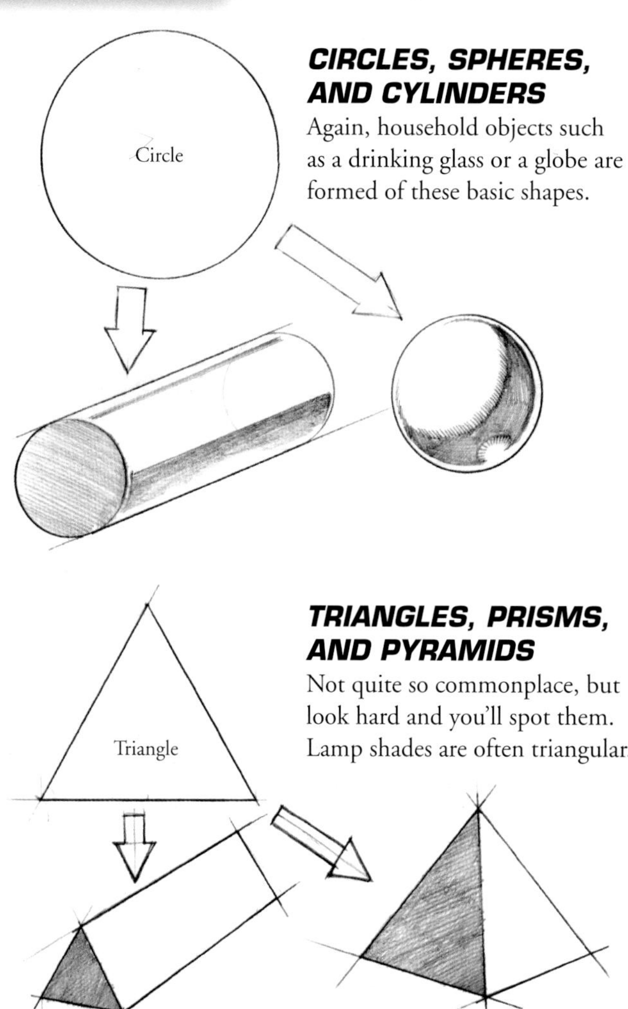

CIRCLES, SPHERES, AND CYLINDERS

Again, household objects such as a drinking glass or a globe are formed of these basic shapes.

TRIANGLES, PRISMS, AND PYRAMIDS

Not quite so commonplace, but look hard and you'll spot them. Lamp shades are often triangular.

SQUARES, CUBES, RECTANGLES, AND CUBOIDS

Many everyday objects are formed of squares and rectangles and their 3-D equivalents: cubes and cuboids. A filing cabinet, a TV set, a briefcase all start life on the page as these basic shapes.

COMMON EXAMPLES OF SHAPES

Here are just a few everyday examples. Before moving onto complex interlocking machine shapes, practice drawing simple, basic objects from all of the above groups. Once you've mastered those, you'll be ready to start combining shapes.

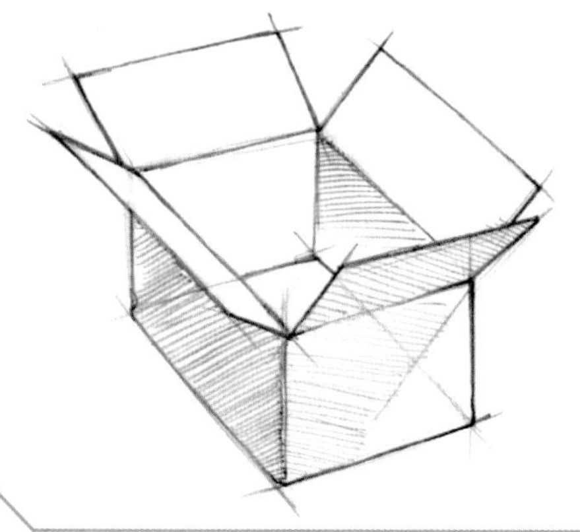

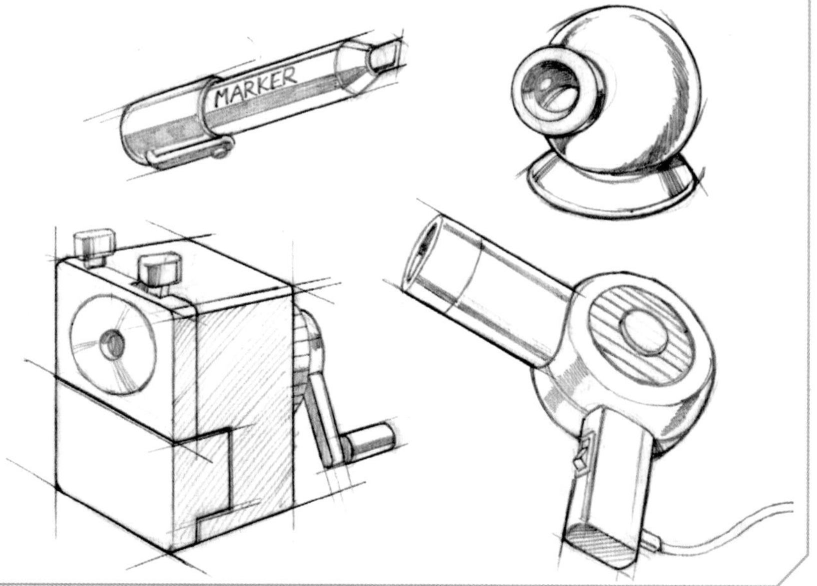

COMBINATIONS

Here's one quick example of forming a more complex illustration from the basic shape groups. The van is assembled, starting with a basic cube, using squares, rectangles, rounded or shaved cuboids, triangles, and circles.

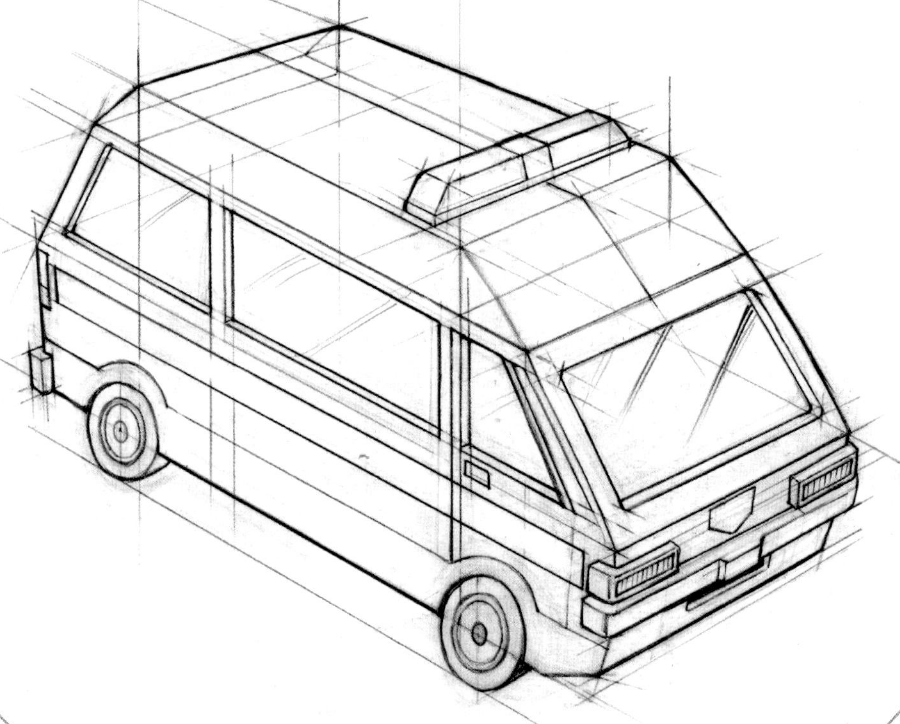

Master the Basics

Shortly, we'll start to see how all but the most humanoid robots are formed of these basic shapes. In the picture above, you can see how the image is made up from cylinders, cones, and circles. In the picture to the above left, the image is made up from elongated cubes and cylinders.

YOUR TURN

Always begin your object with the most obvious or simple shape, be it a cube, a sphere, or a pyramid, sketched in lightly using a 4H or even a 6H pencil. Then start to refine the shape, curving or cutting edges as necessary, before adding other shapes. Then, using your art pencil(s) of choice, add in the detail and shading.

BASIC FIGURE

THE ROBOT FORM

As with the human form, a basic upright robotic figure should start life as a stick figure. This will provide a solid foundation on which to build your more detailed illustration, as well as helping you with the figure's specific pose and general proportions. It's worth thinking of robots, first and foremost, as human beings with armor plating.

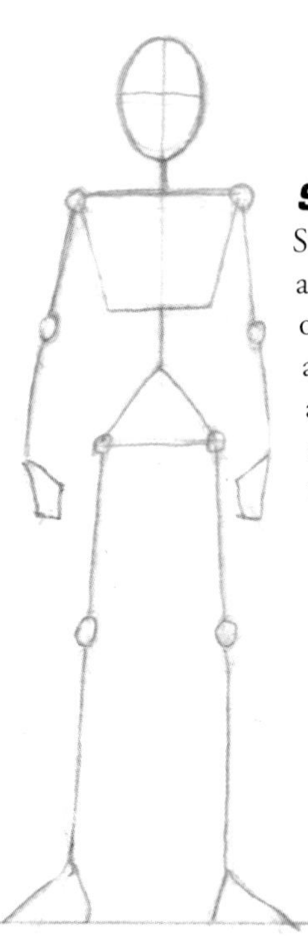

Stick Figure
Start with the head and sketch in a spine or central axis. Then add jointed arms and legs, using simple shapes for the main torso.

Human
Add very basic musculature and definition to the figure. Sketch lightly, as much of this line work will be erased as you add armor.

TRANSFORMER
Refer back to your vehicular (or other) alternative mode and turn smooth and organic lines into angular robotic detail.

PRACTICE MAKES PERFECT

See how much dynamism is introduced into the three figures (right) with just a very slight manipulation of the more standard static pose. Practice by reversing the process (above) and stripping these finished figures back to simple stick figure sketches.

Shockwave

Rodimus Prime

Grimlock

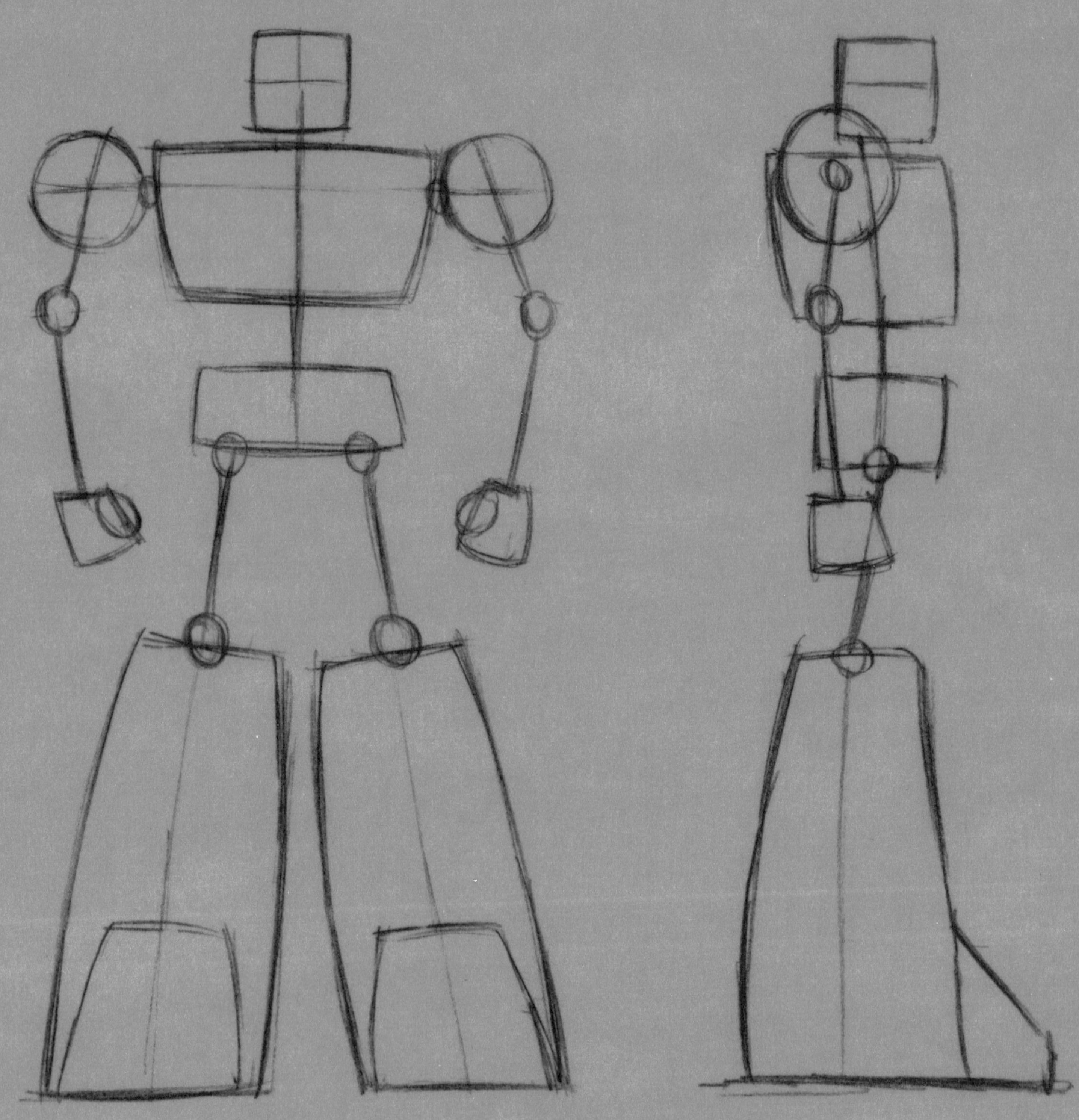

DIMENSIONS

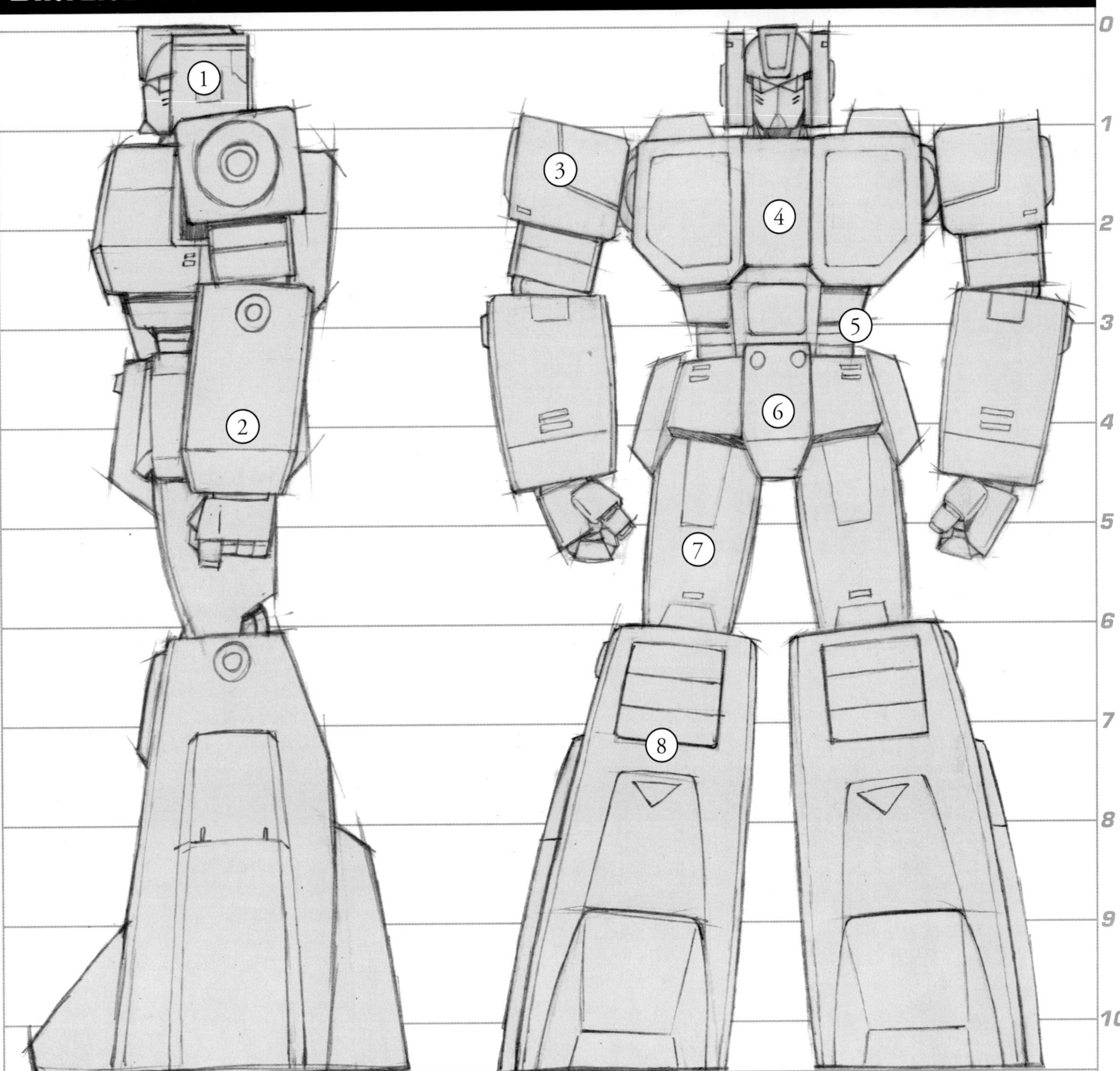

1. Figures are measured in '"heads" (literally the height of one head). Draw your proportion grid accordingly.
2. An arm is roughly four heads long and begins above the main torso (remember the neck).
3. Using very basic shapes, add the shoulder segments. By their nature, robots are at their widest at this point.
4. Work down through the chest and trunk area, adding shape and detail. Start wide…
5. … and then narrow things down as you approach the waist. Use your rough human musculature as a guide.
6. Bulk out the armor at the waist, creating "hips." Shoulder to waist is approximately three heads.
7. Upper leg segments are two heads. Note that the hand ends midway through this measurement.
8. Add lower legs and feet to "ground" level. Indicate the knees (of a human figure) with detailing.

VARIATIONS

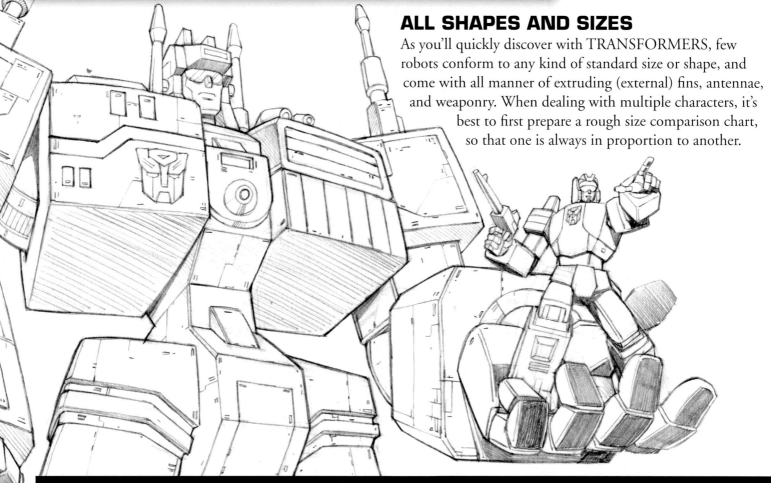

ALL SHAPES AND SIZES

As you'll quickly discover with TRANSFORMERS, few robots conform to any kind of standard size or shape, and come with all manner of extruding (external) fins, antennae, and weaponry. When dealing with multiple characters, it's best to first prepare a rough size comparison chart, so that one is always in proportion to another.

BODY TYPES

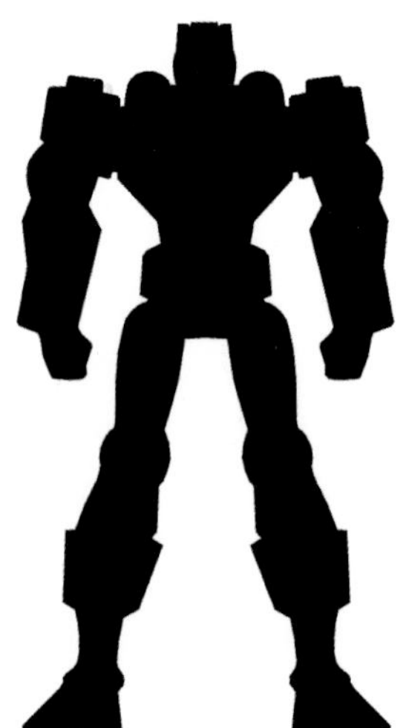

Humanoid: Such characters are closest to a standard human figure, and therefore have defined musculature rather than bulky body segments.

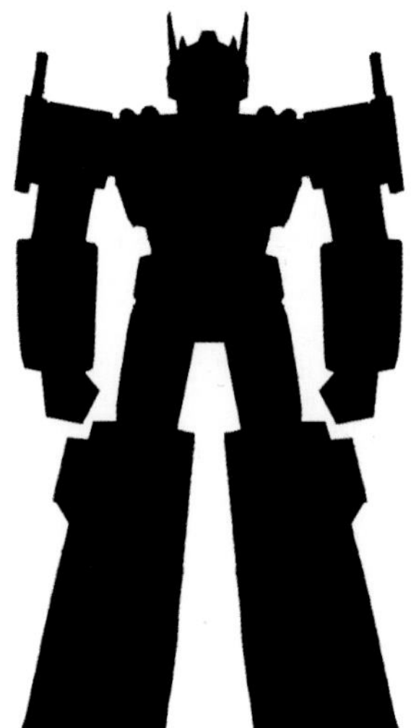

Medium build: One stage up from the humanoid figure, with more blocky body segments providing extra bulk and girth. This limits the available action poses.

Oversized: The real bruisers of the TRANSFORMERS universe are those with non-standard and unconventional alternative forms. They are often bulky and awkward in action.

TIPS

Not all TRANSFORMERS have the same proportions. You can play with the basic shapes in order to create different kinds of robots. For example, a smaller head or bigger arms may suggest a bulkier robot, while longers legs may add a dynamic feel. Some characters, like Bumblebee, may have a slightly bigger head so to appear "younger" than others.
Guido Guidi

Arcee

Note how the designers have modeled Arcee on a human female (instead of the more standard male) form. Here, the humanoid model is most suitable for the character, as it allows for ease of movement and sleek appearance. Even Arcee's vehicular mode is designed to enhance her sense of speed and grace.

Scorponok

A very complex alternative mode leads to a highly detailed and busy robot mode. Everything here says massive and monolithic, from the heavy two-toed feet to the claws and armaments.

Sideswipe

Here's an excellent example of a solid, blocky (medium build) character, one whose robot form consciously ditches style and maneuverability in favour of imposing body mass and dense armature.

VEHICLES

STEP-BY-STEP

Now you can draw basic figures, let's look at the vehicles they transform into.

1) Start with a stretched pyramid shape and shave off the point. This is Sunstreaker's main chassis.

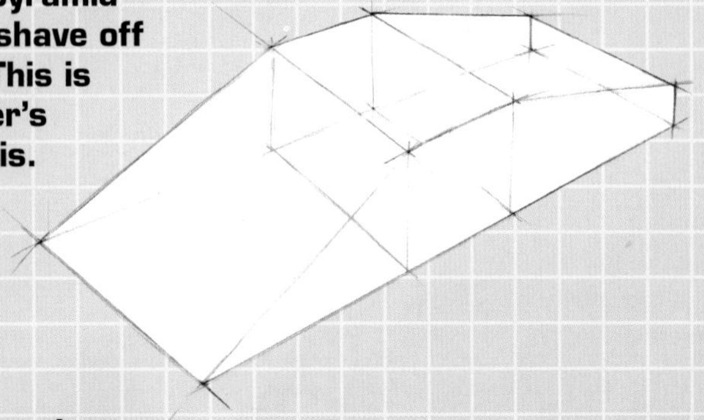

SHAPING UP

Sunstreaker is based on a Lamborghini LP500S. Often with science fiction/fantasy, vehicles are plucked from the artist's imagination, but TRANSFORMERS generally turn into real vehicles. Always have appropriate reference material to hand before you start drawing and then start to consider the core shapes at work in the design.

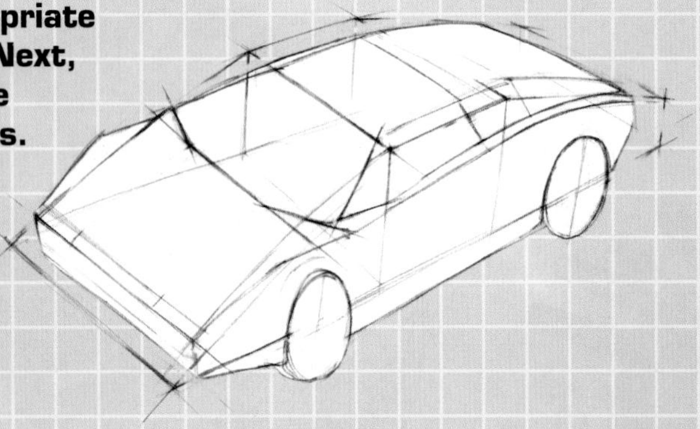

3) Add more specific detail, including the headlights, rear cut away section, and spoiler.

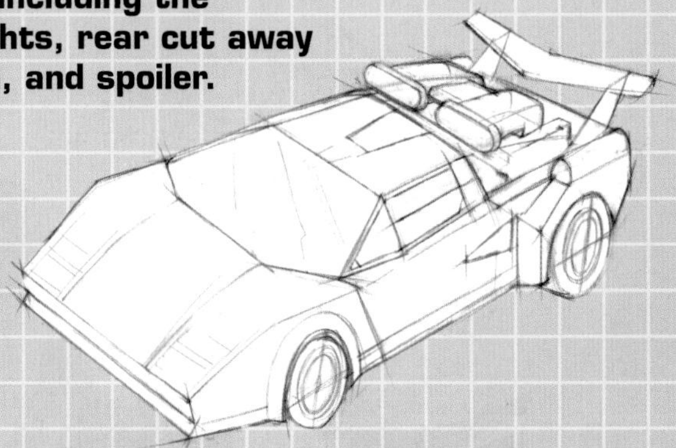

2) Curve the sharp edges of the roof and sketch in the windows (using appropriate reference). Next, sketch in the visible wheels.

4) Finally, start to tighten up (define) your pencil lines. Consider the smaller detailing on the vehicle, such items as wing mirrors and wheel trims, and add shading where necessary.

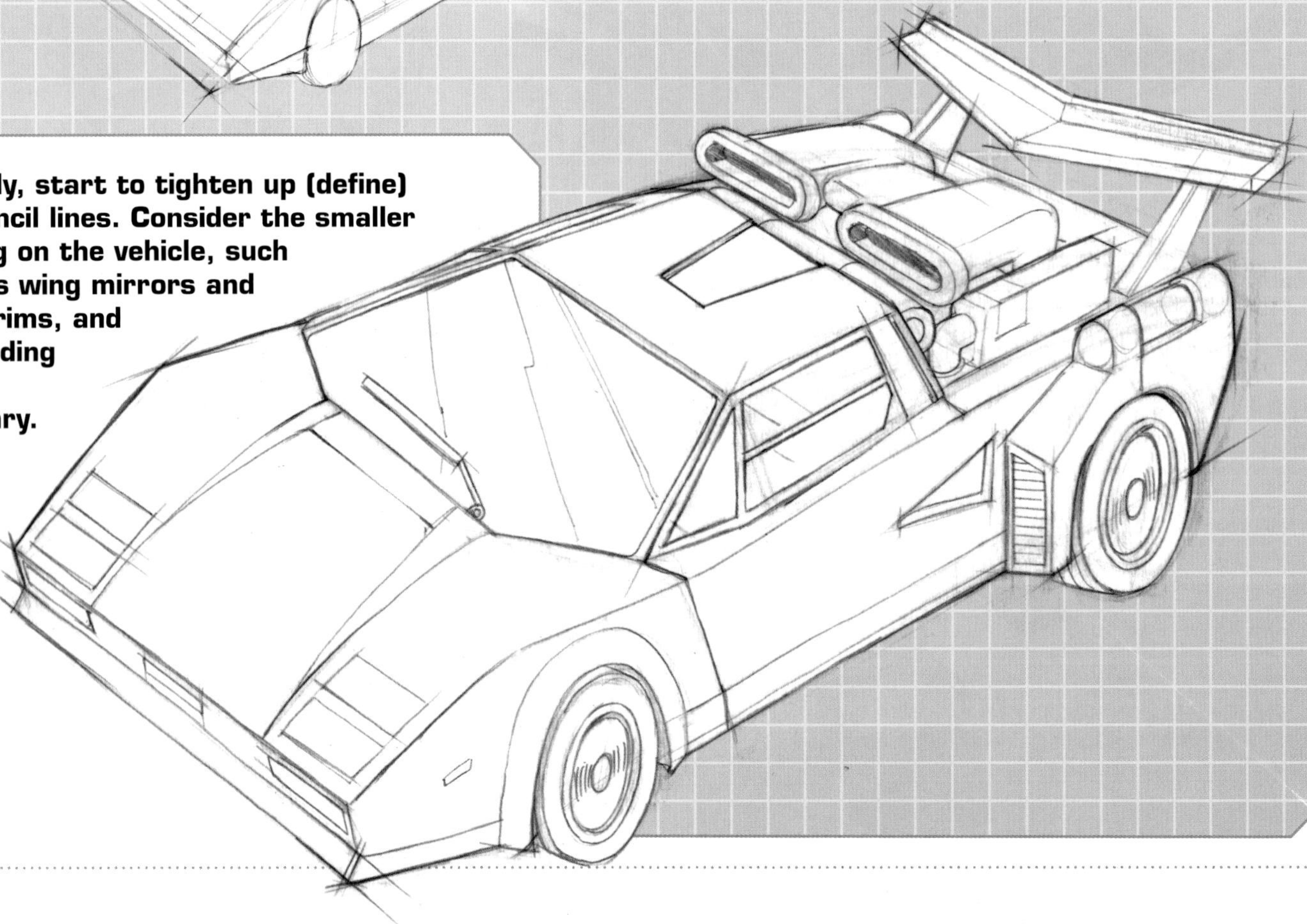

1) Starscream is based on a F-15 fighter jet. Use rectangles, triangles, and an elliptical (stretched circle) shape (for the nosecone/ cockpit section).

2) Once the shapes are interlocked to your satisfaction, start to add in details such as the tail fins and under-wing weaponry.

3) Using your reference material, refine the rough sketch further. Shape the wings, cockpit, and the nosecone more precisely.

4) Erase any superfluous or unwanted line work and tighten up your pencils, adding extra detail and shading, motion lines or (as here) thruster jets flaring.

TIPS

When drawing alternate modes that exist in real life, don't be afraid to use photographic references. Be sure to draw each vehicle from multiple angles so you fully understand the vehicle's basic shapes, and to have a complete view of the main details, such as lights, grilles, wheels, or wings.

Guido Guidi

PERSPECTIVE

ENVIRONMENTS

Once you've mastered basic figure drawing, the next step is to provide suitable environments for the characters. This means learning about perspective, which applies a three-dimensional aspect to flat (2-D) line drawing. Backgrounds and buildings need angles and depth to fool the eye, and some relatively simple rules apply.

HORIZON

The further away a character is, the smaller he or she appears. The last point at which they can be seen is the horizon. This straight line is the starting point of perspective.

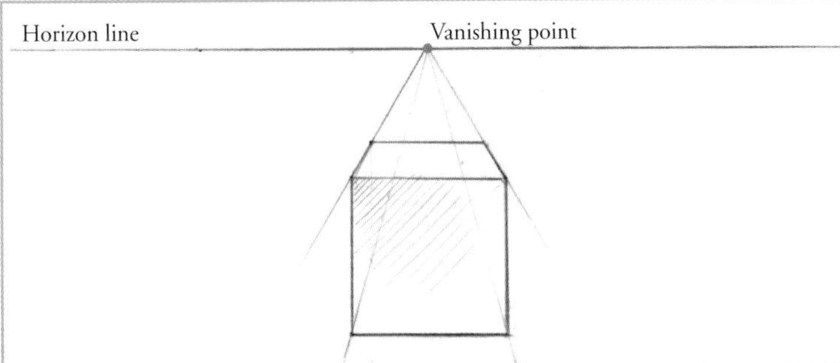

VANISHING POINT

Consider a box. At eye-level it appears as a flat square or rectangle. Lower the box slightly below eye level and the top becomes visible. Look closer and the top appears to get narrower towards the back. Extend the left and right edges of the box top into the distance. The lines get closer and closer and eventually connect at the horizon line. This is the vanishing point.

Vanishing point
Horizon line
Vanishing point

TWO-POINT PERSPECTIVE

With the box still slightly below eye-level, rotate it a half turn so that you can now see the top and two of its sides. See how all three sides narrow towards the background. Consider the left edges and extend them to a vanishing point on the left. Then extend the right edges to a vanishing point on the right. This is a two-point perspective. The same applies if you lift the box above eye-level.

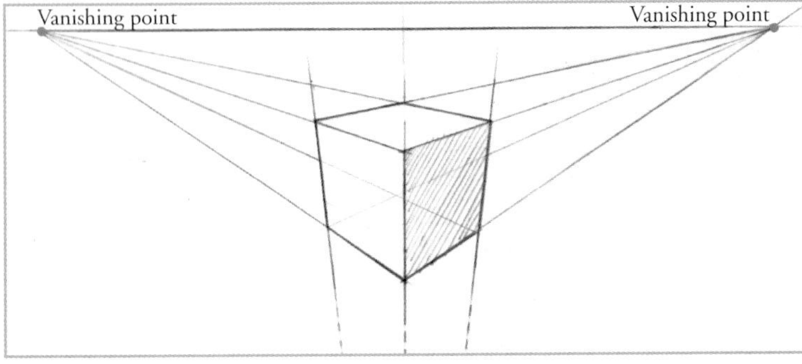

THREE-POINT PERSPECTIVE

Raise or lower the box an inch or two more. You can start to see the uprights narrow slightly, and if you extended those lines enough (though you'd need a very large piece of paper) they would eventually meet at a third vanishing point, above or below. This three-point perspective is used to give height or depth to your picture.

PERSPECTIVE IN SCENES

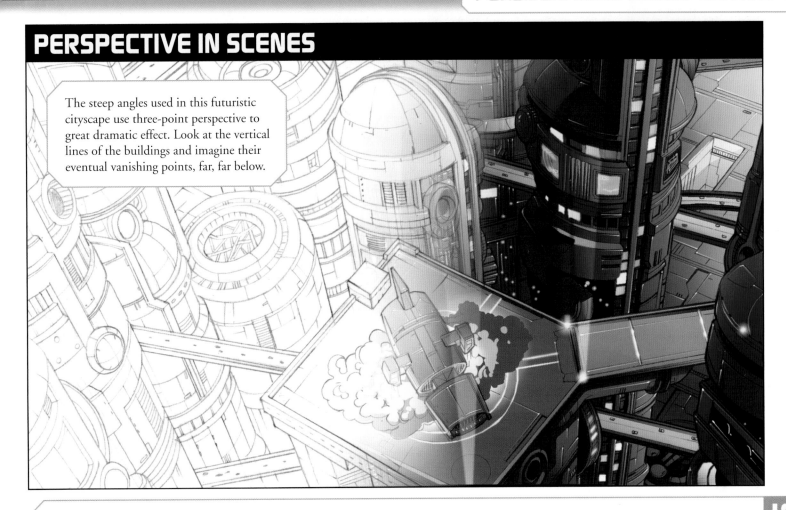

The steep angles used in this futuristic cityscape use three-point perspective to great dramatic effect. Look at the vertical lines of the buildings and imagine their eventual vanishing points, far, far below.

STEP-BY-STEP

COMPOSITION

Perspective also comes into its own when creating backgrounds that add to or enhance your figure drawing. Compose these two elements early on for the best effect:

1) Create the corridor walls and ceiling using a horizon line and a vanishing point. Draw as many lines as you need to create the scene and then position your figure centrally.

2) Sketch in more detail, such as paneling and strip lighting on the walls and ceiling and add a door at the end of the corridor. Then tighten up the line work on the central figure.

3) Erase the vanishing point and perspective guidelines and fully render the character and corridor. You can see how the dramatic angle of the background aids the impression of motion in the figure.

BODY PERSPECTIVE

DRAMATIC FIGUREWORK

Earlier, in the basic figure drawing section, we kept our given perspective on a character conventional in the extreme. To add dramatic effect to a character or to suggest a viewpoint other than eye-level, three-point perspective again comes into its own. The same rules that apply to buildings and boxes apply equally to figure work, with the careful application of overlaid perspective lines and vanishing points.

UP SHOT/DOWN SHOT

Take a look at these two images. The top image is framed in a fairly conventional manner, at, or maybe just below eye-level. In the lower image the perspective has changed dramatically, and we're looking down at the character from above. This is called a down shot. The reverse is an up shot, giving dramatic height and stature to a character (as with Optimus Prime, left).

SKETCHBOOK

EVERY WHICH WAY

Here, the artist has taken one character and applied a mixed bag of different perspective points and angles. Practice by taking a sheet of tracing paper and adding in the perspective lines that apply to each different pose. Or, select a character of your choice and either duplicate the poses shown here or, if you're feeling confident, try and select alternative poses and angles.

TRANSFORMING

THE BASICS

Transforming a character from a robot into the alternative mode (or vice versa) is the most challenging aspect of drawing TRANSFORMERS. As mentioned earlier, the best way to work out what goes where and how the various sections interlock or separate is to reverse the process, from vehicle (or whatever) to robot.

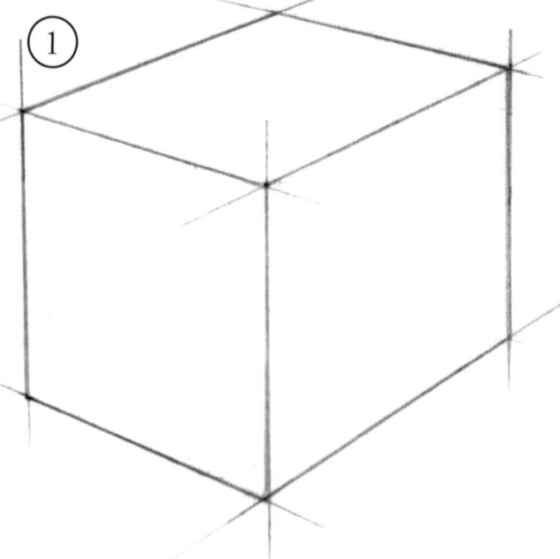

1) Draw a straightforward outline cube, with three sides showing (remember your two-point perspective).

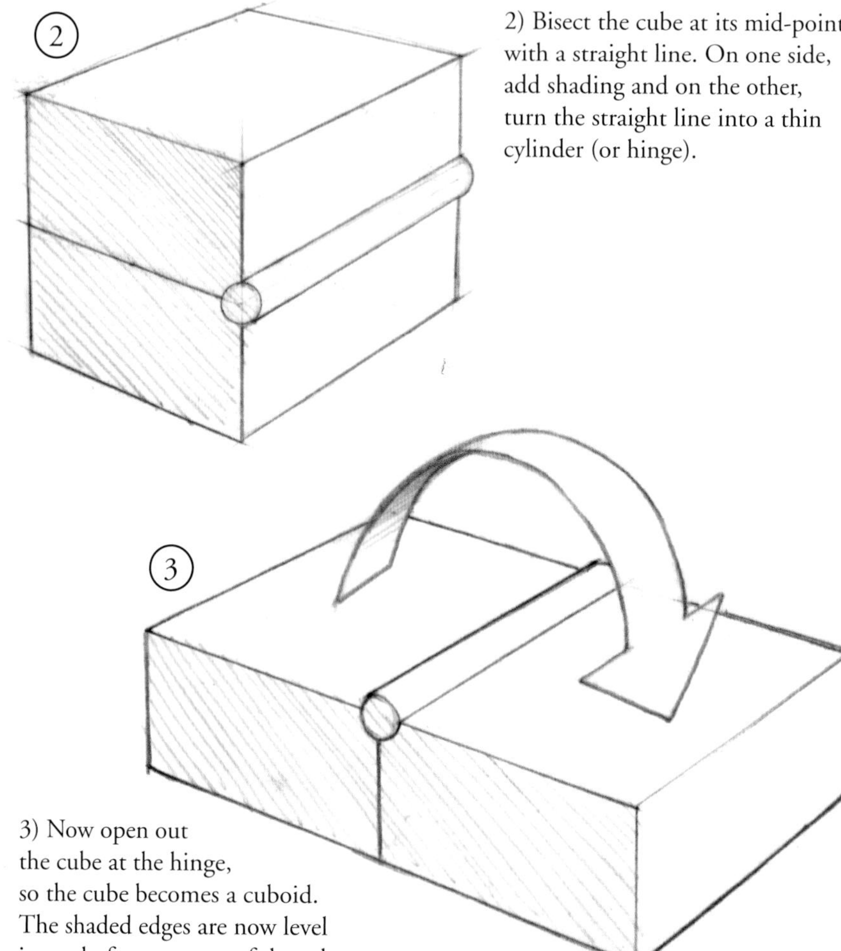

2) Bisect the cube at its mid-point with a straight line. On one side, add shading and on the other, turn the straight line into a thin cylinder (or hinge).

3) Now open out the cube at the hinge, so the cube becomes a cuboid. The shaded edges are now level instead of one on top of the other.

EXERCISE

Consider this fairly complex transformation sequence and try and work out which sections of the jet become which sections of the robot, and which areas pivot, twist, rotate, tuck, or extend in the process (more on this on pages 26–27).

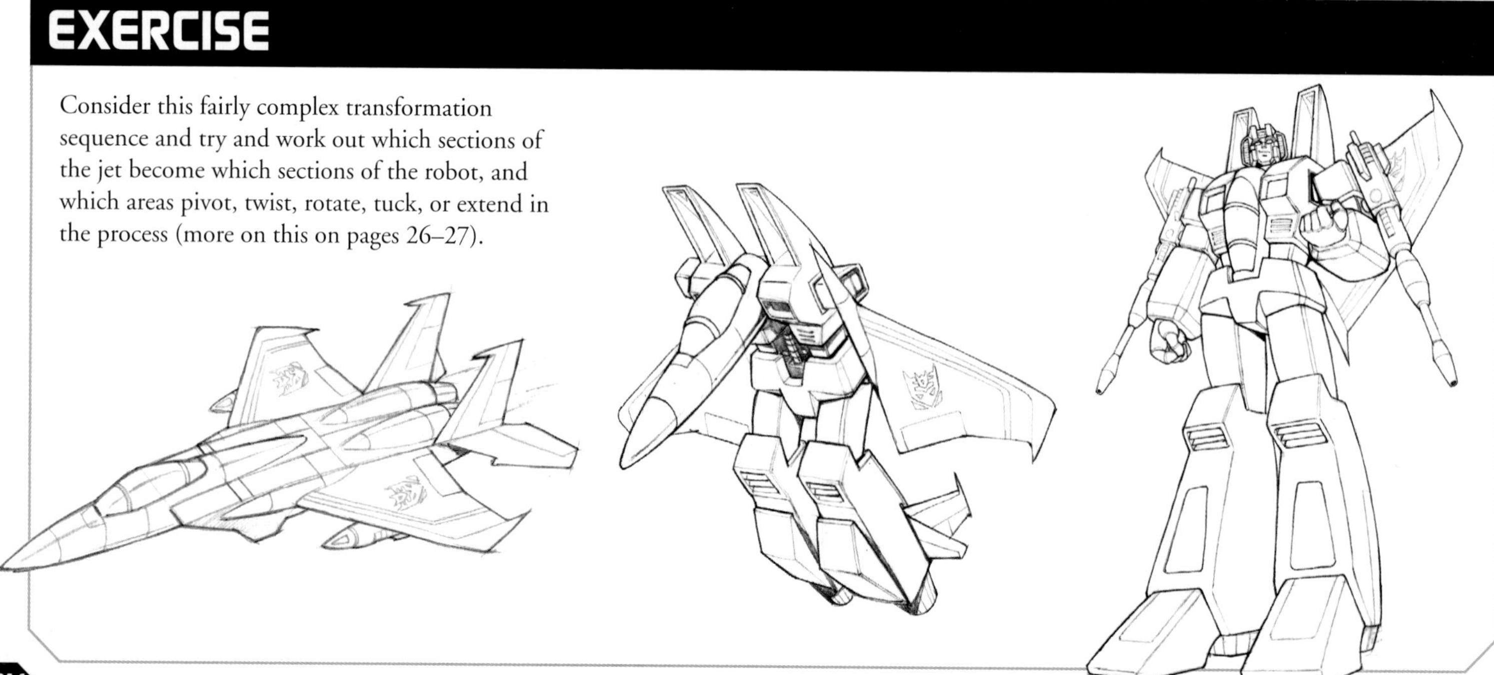

NEXT STAGE

Now we're going to take another shape and consider two different ways it can be manipulated, this time to form upper or lower limbs and body parts. Then, we'll take that process and apply it to an actual TRANSFORMER.

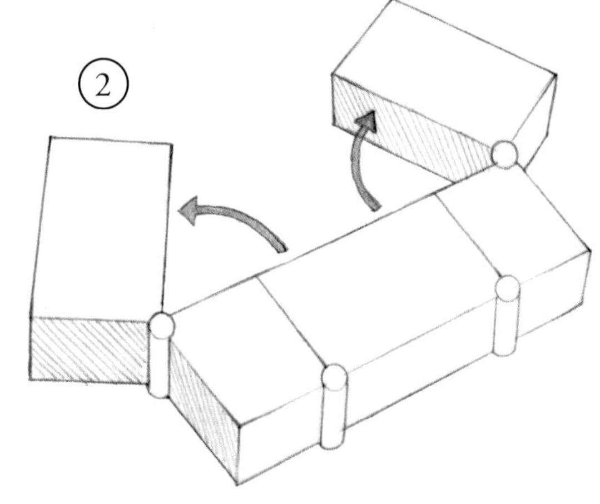

2) Open out the two halves of the top segment, leaving the lower segment intact (and picture an upper torso with arms)...

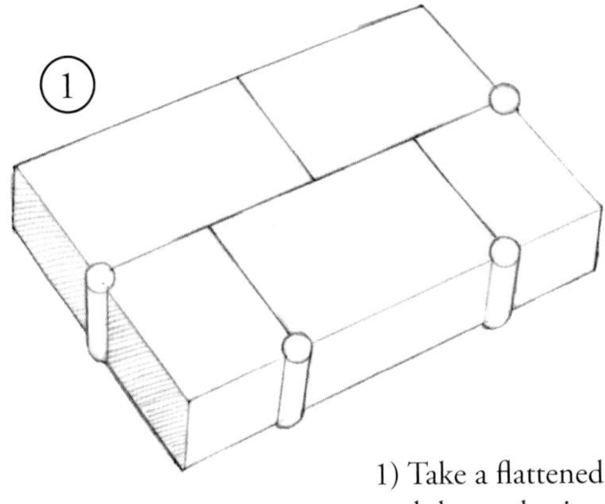

1) Take a flattened cuboid and draw a horizontal line that cuts it in two. Divide the top half into two, and the bottom half into three. Add hinges on the left and right and two on the bottom.

3

3) ...then open the lower two hinges and bring the left and right sections of the lower segment down, bringing the top two with them (and imagine lower trunk and legs).

STEP-BY-STEP

FRENZY
We can now take the basic principles and apply them to an actual character, namely the Decepticon mini-cassette/robot Frenzy:

1) Draw a flattened cuboid. Add in the detailing and identify the sections that need to separate.

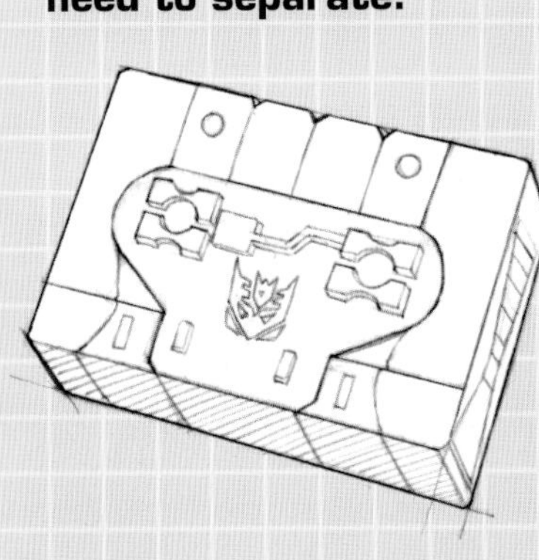

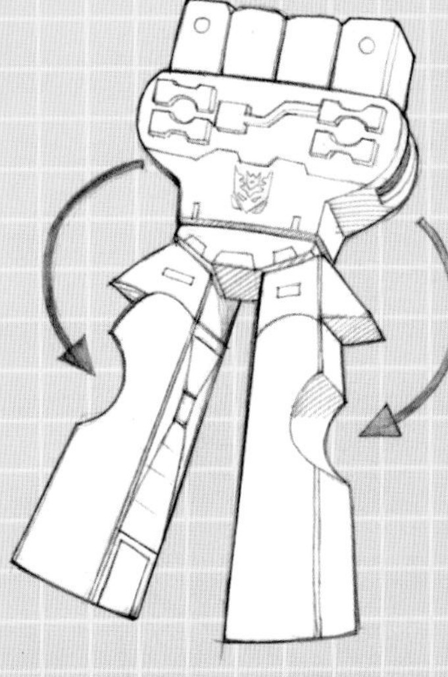

2) Move the outer (leg) sections out and down and rotate them outwards, so the feet are foremost.

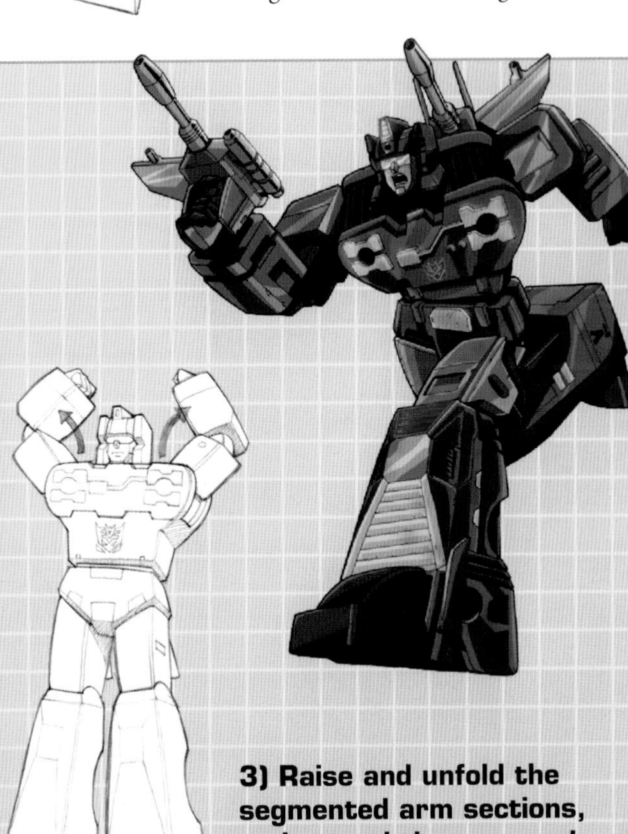

3) Raise and unfold the segmented arm sections, and extend the recessed head and hands.

TWISTS AND TURNS

The transformation process involves often convoluted twists and turns, full rotations, tucks, and extensions. Other than in the instructions that accompany each toy, the whole process is seldom illustrated from start to finish (and without some dramatic licence), but certain maneuvers are worth practicing nonetheless.

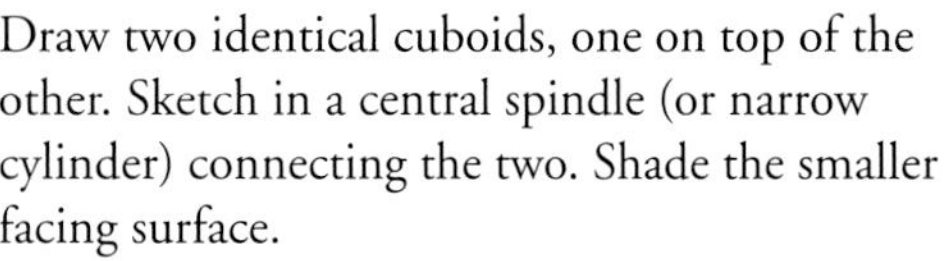

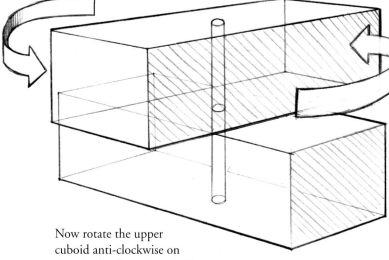

Draw two identical cuboids, one on top of the other. Sketch in a central spindle (or narrow cylinder) connecting the two. Shade the smaller facing surface.

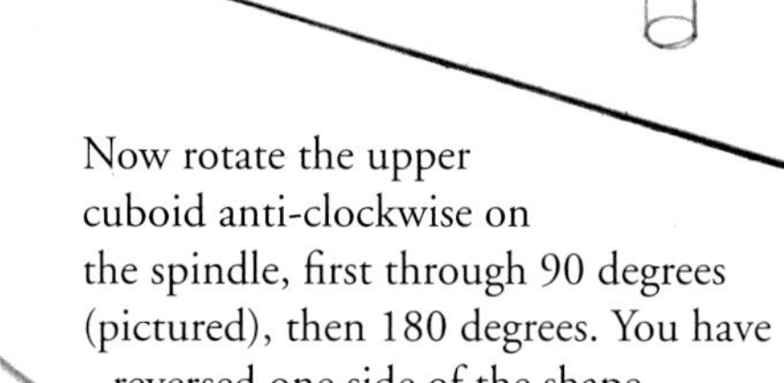

Now rotate the upper cuboid anti-clockwise on the spindle, first through 90 degrees (pictured), then 180 degrees. You have reversed one side of the shape.

ROTATION

Often, whole body sections are rotated and reversed during the transformation sequence. Here, the robot rotates at the waist, lower body turning through 180 degrees so that the retractable feet are now facing front and ready for extension. The process is reversed when the robot begins its transformation to alt. (alternative) mode.

EXTENSIONS

Many robots have telescoping limbs, whereby one or more sections of the arm or leg are stored (in alt. mode) in special cavities in the adjoining segment. In this fashion, not all elements of the robot are visible while in alt. mode, and vice versa.

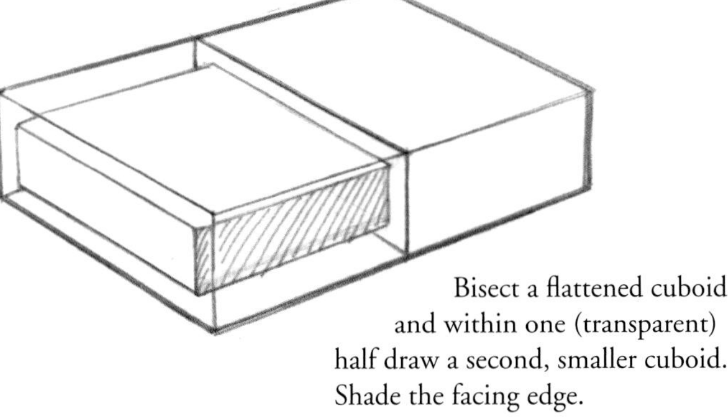

Bisect a flattened cuboid and within one (transparent) half draw a second, smaller cuboid. Shade the facing edge.

Here, a hand is recessed within a hollow cavity in the lower arm and extended on transformation to robot mode.

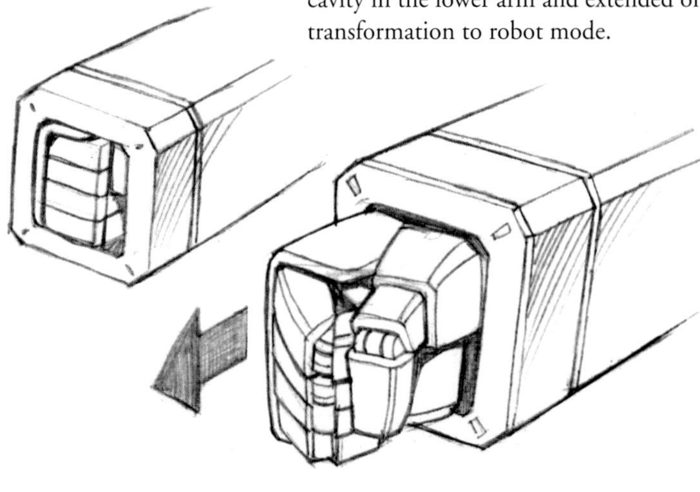

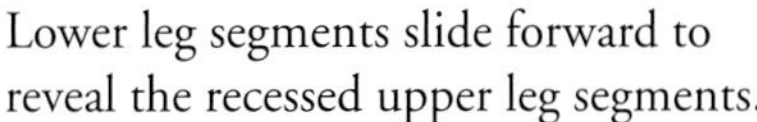

Lower leg segments slide forward to reveal the recessed upper leg segments.

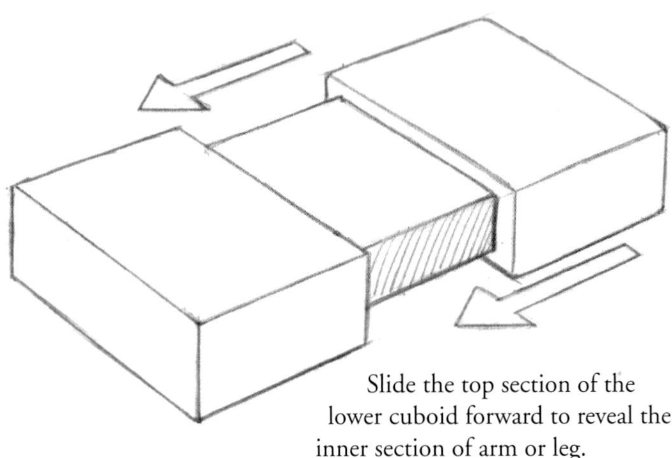

Slide the top section of the lower cuboid forward to reveal the inner section of arm or leg.

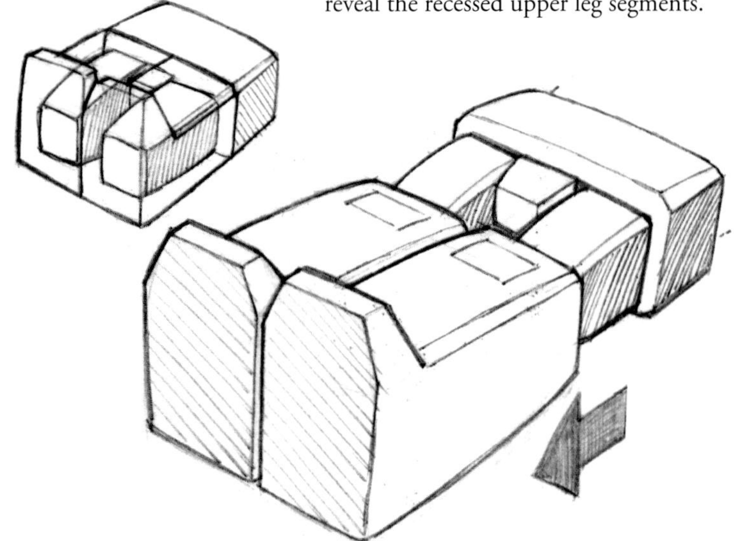

FOLDOUT LIMBS

In some robots the lower segment of arm is contained within the upper segment and instead of being extended on a sliding mechanism…

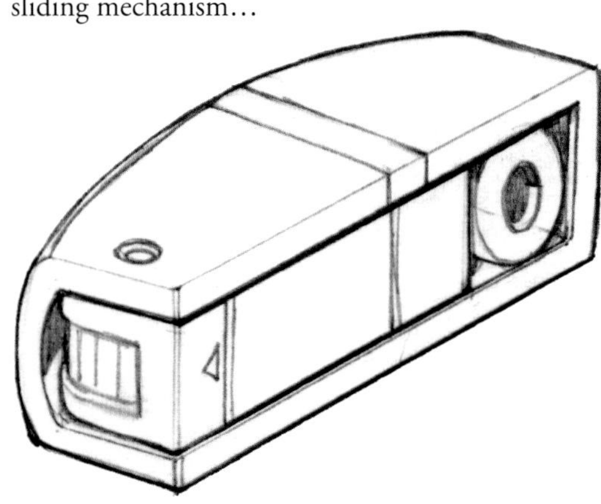

…flips or folds out when the upper arm is moved away from the body. The hand is then extended from its recessed cavity.

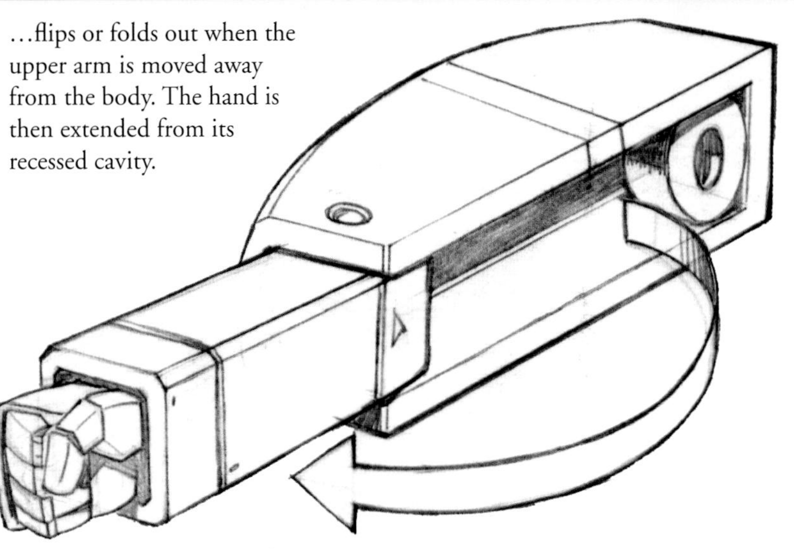

FULL TRANSFORMATION

Now let's take a character (in this case, diminutive Autobot super-spy Bumblebee) through a full transformation sequence. Previously in this section we've identified the various elements that come together in both straightforward and complex transformations and now we can see them in free-flowing action as vehicle becomes robot in five distinct stages.

1. We start in vehicle mode. Bumblebee is modeled on a classic Volkswagen Beetle. At this stage, identify which elements of the car become what parts of the upright robot and plan accordingly.

2. The front (hood) section extends to become the feet, revealing the telescoping upper and lower legs. Note how the character springs forward, adding motion and dramatic impact to the transformation.

3. The wheels rotate inwards into cavities, revealing the arms. Hands and head extend from recessed areas. The roof of the car/chest remains static throughout.

4. As we reach robot mode the arms and legs separate and become more animated. The character is now almost ready to spring into action, his Autobot chest insignia prominent.

5. Finally, Bumblebee is armed and ready for battle. Though none exist on the toys themselves, artists have introduced recessed cavities for the robots' hand-held weaponry, and sometimes the blaster or energy sword is released early on in the transformation sequence, and caught in robot mode.

TIPS

To make the robot's transformation more dynamic, I like to exaggerate each step. On the last step I pay close attention to the eyes, making them glow as if the robot has been activated into life after transforming.

Marcelo Matere

SHADING & LIGHTING

HIGHLIGHTS AND LOWLIGHTS

The dramatic intensity or mood of a scene can be enhanced by shading, giving depth and dimension to flat line work. To understand how and where to apply shading, it's important to consider from what direction the primary light source is coming.

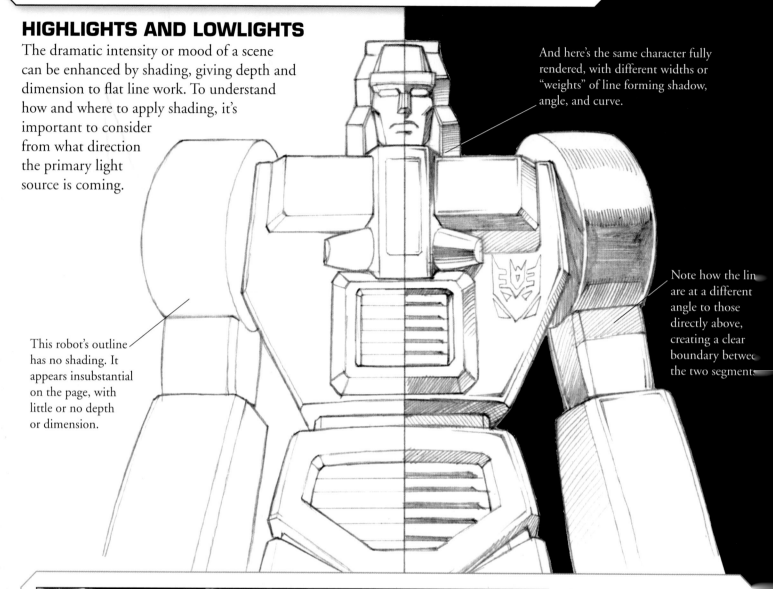

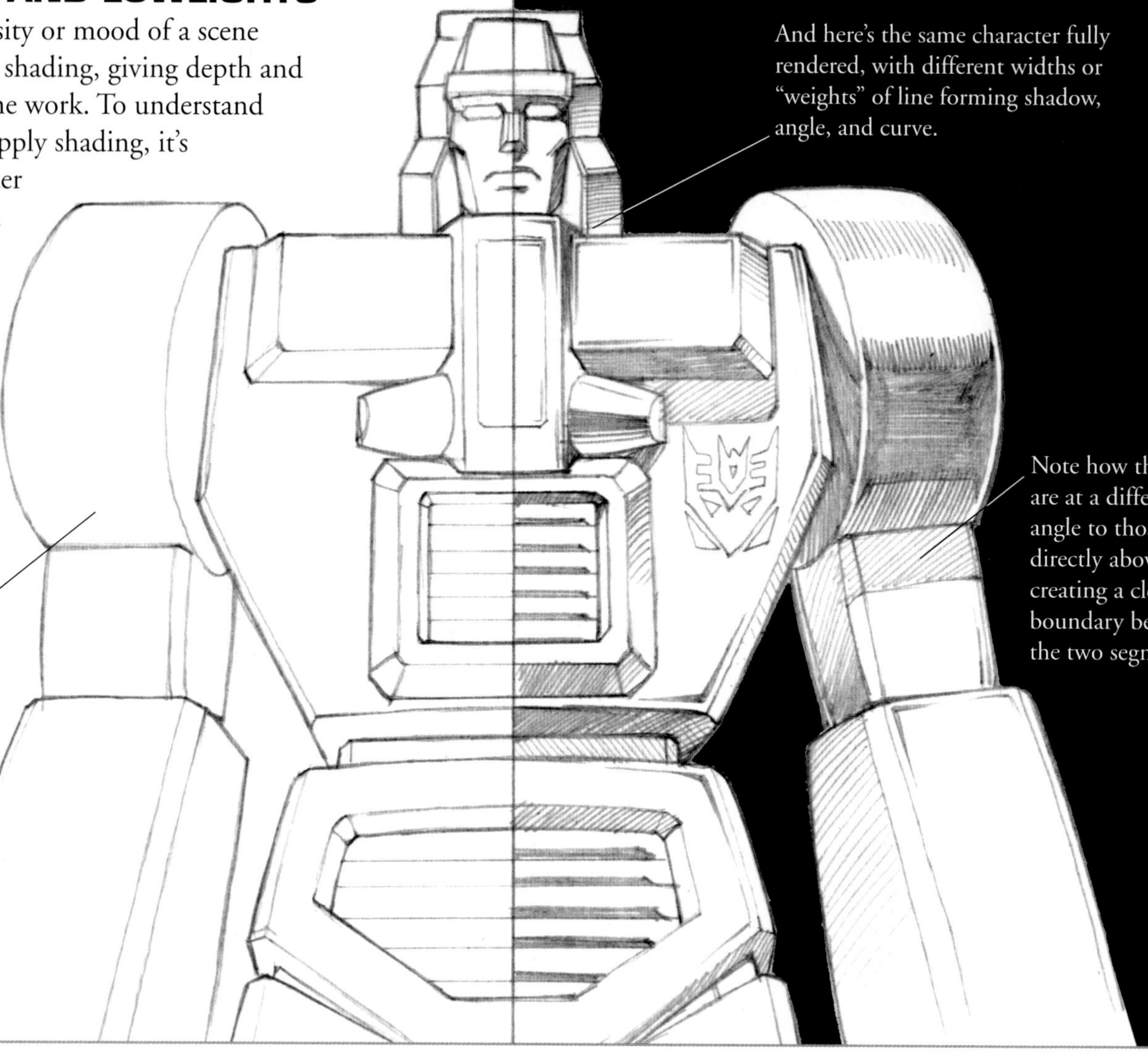

And here's the same character fully rendered, with different widths or "weights" of line forming shadow, angle, and curve.

Note how the lin are at a different angle to those directly above, creating a clear boundary betwe the two segment

This robot's outline has no shading. It appears insubstantial on the page, with little or no depth or dimension.

MOOD

In this dramatic image from TRANSFORMERS Armada, the figure of Megatron is uplit by fires to striking effect. The body, bent forwards in this manner, absorbs most of the direct light (from off, below), so the face is plunged into moody, menacing dark shadow. Within this area of darkness, the eyes burn bright giving Megatron an almost demonic aspect. See how the artist and colorist have used one element of the scene to enhance the character within it.

LIGHT SOURCES

Here we have four images of exactly the same head but lit from four different directions. The shadows deepen and intensify in some and become diffused or lighter in others, creating an entirely different aspect to the character.

Here, the head (left) is uplit, with the light source directly under the face. The intense, dark shadows gather above the cheek lines and around the eyes, giving an eerie or foreboding appearance to the character.

In the sketch above, the light source is coming from the right, so the shadows fall on the left-hand side of the face. The reverse effect (light source coming from the left) can be seen above, right.

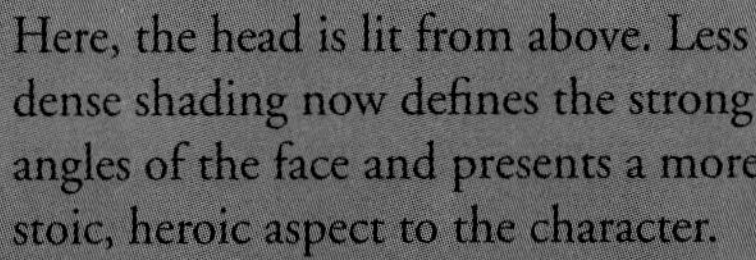

Here, the head is lit from above. Less dense shading now defines the strong angles of the face and presents a more stoic, heroic aspect to the character.

TIPS

Shine a desk lamp on some household objects (even your TRANSFORMERS toys!) and draw what you see. Sketching real objects in different types of lighting makes you pay attention to how shadows fall. With this practice, it will become easier for you to add shade and depth to your TRANSFORMERS drawings.

Nick Roche

FORESHORTENING

IN YOUR FACE

Foreshortening is a visual effect or optical illusion that suggests that an object or distance is shorter than it actually appears because it is angled towards the viewer.

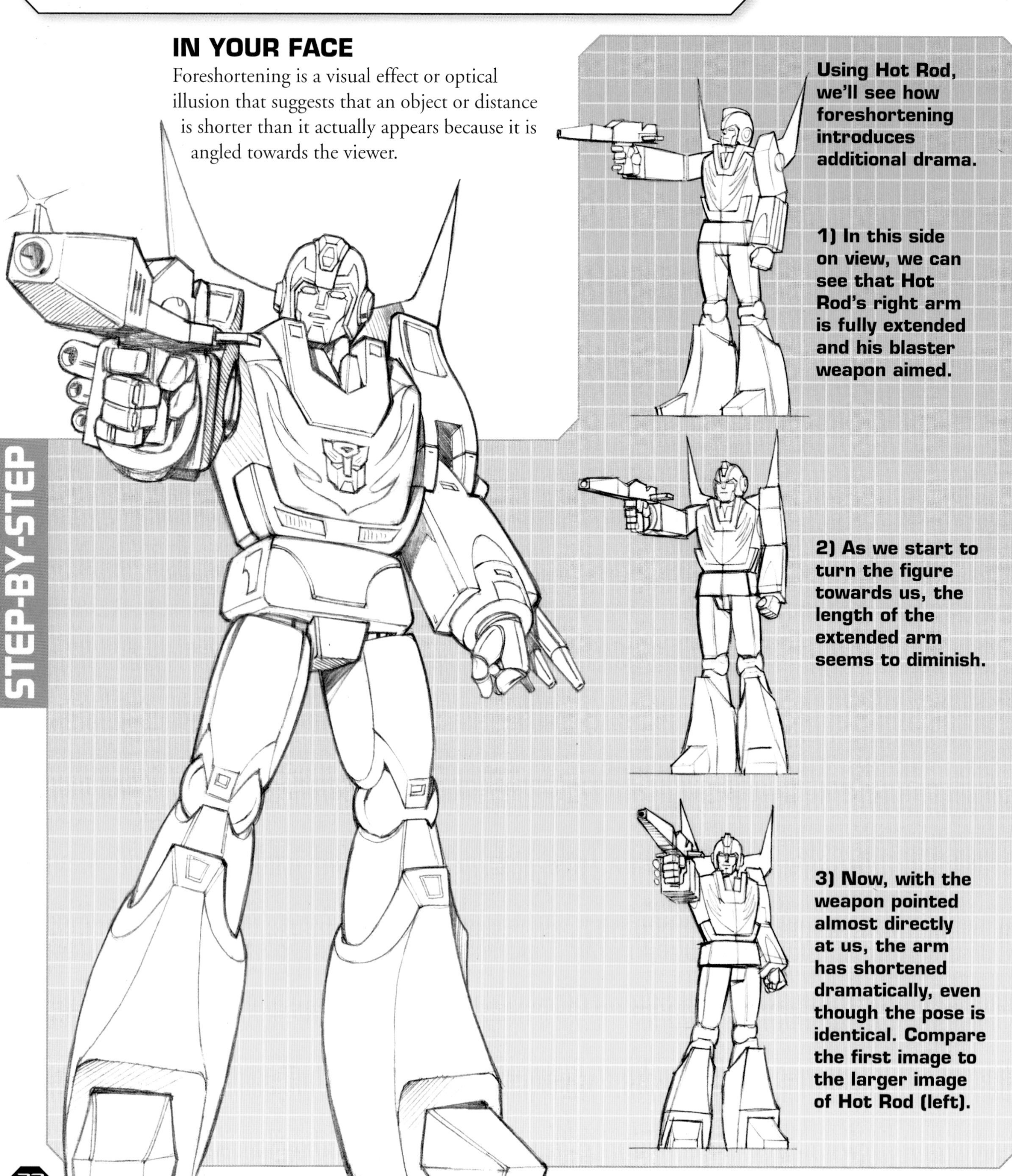

Using Hot Rod, we'll see how foreshortening introduces additional drama.

1) In this side on view, we can see that Hot Rod's right arm is fully extended and his blaster weapon aimed.

2) As we start to turn the figure towards us, the length of the extended arm seems to diminish.

3) Now, with the weapon pointed almost directly at us, the arm has shortened dramatically, even though the pose is identical. Compare the first image to the larger image of Hot Rod (left).

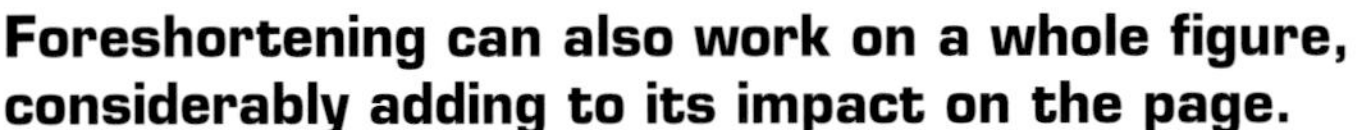

Foreshortening can also work on a whole figure, considerably adding to its impact on the page.

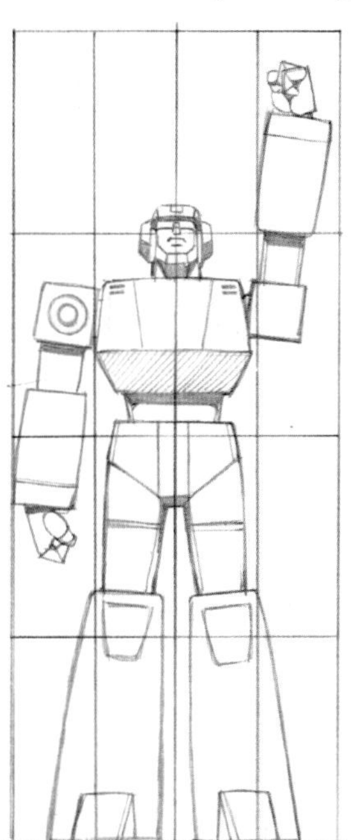

1) Start with an upright figure and draw a grid pattern with the feet on the base line.

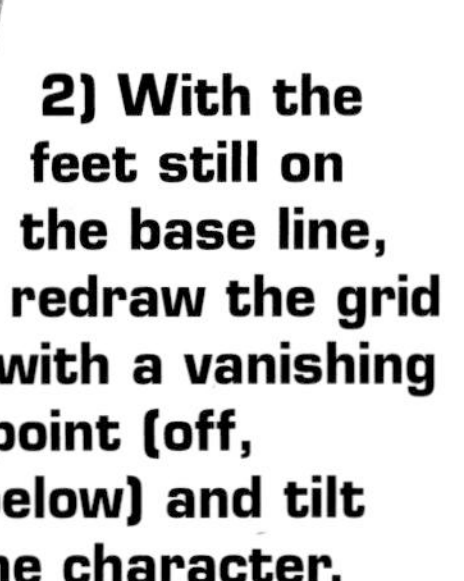

2) With the feet still on the base line, redraw the grid with a vanishing point (off, below) and tilt the character.

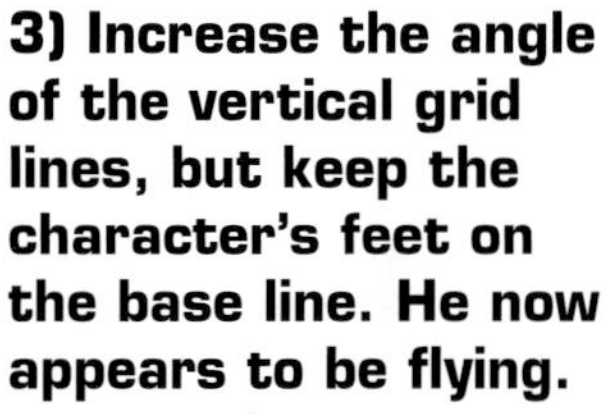

3) Increase the angle of the vertical grid lines, but keep the character's feet on the base line. He now appears to be flying.

One Giant Leap

Here's an excellent example of foreshortening from the first volume of *The War Within.* Look at the way Megatron is almost bursting out of the page, his hands seemingly reaching right out at the reader.

TIPS

Once you have established the angle that you are going to use for your image, exaggerate the proportions as if the "camera" has moved closer to the object. A large hand in the foreground and smaller feet in the distance will add drama and impact. Also, adjust the pose of the figure so that it really leans into the camera.

Andrew Wildman

ACTION!

READY, SET... GO!

So far, we've concentrated largely on static poses, but the true art of the TRANSFORMERS lies in turning these images into explosive action on the page. That means we need to consider how these characters move. If they're running, for example, what happens to their arms? As so often, observation and practice make perfect!

WHAM-BAM!

In this scene, as Optimus Prime punches, so his torso twists. The blow causes Megatron to recoil from the impact; his back arches, and he unclenches his own fist on reflex.

STEP-BY-STEP

The best way to animate characters is to take a simple, stripped down figure through some basic exercises while considering every aspect of bodily movement. First, draw an outline figure with defined circles at each of the main joints.

1) Let's start our figure running. As the right leg comes forward, the left leg is lifted. The left arm is raised to chest level, the other is behind.

2) As the left leg starts to come forward, the right leg takes the full weight of the body. The right arm now comes forward.

ACTION SKETCHBOOK

Now sketch an assortment of action poses, still with the same basic figure, and start to add more overtly robotic elements to them. Most robots are jointed in the same way as a human being, so the same poses apply, but you'll find that some actions appear awkward.

3) As the pace increases, so the angle of the propeling leg increases, the body leans forward more, and the knees raise higher.

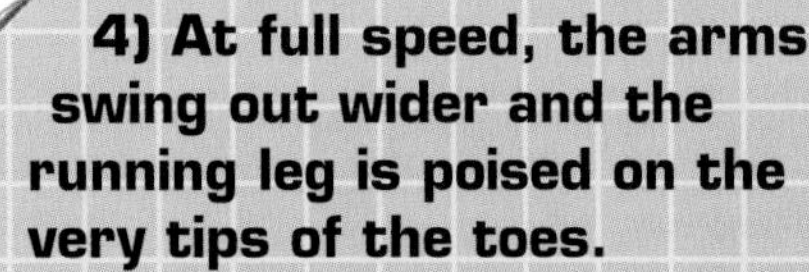

4) At full speed, the arms swing out wider and the running leg is poised on the very tips of the toes.

And Back Again

Now try reversing the action and repeat this whole exercise for jumping, diving, or charging.

BATTLE!

GET READY TO RUMBLE!

We're not expecting you to be able to assemble a battle scene like this (just yet), but it's about time we let our TRANSFORMERS mix it up and while we're at it, reveal how a scene like this goes from rough sketch to finished art. By the time you finish reading this book, you too could be creating scenes like this!

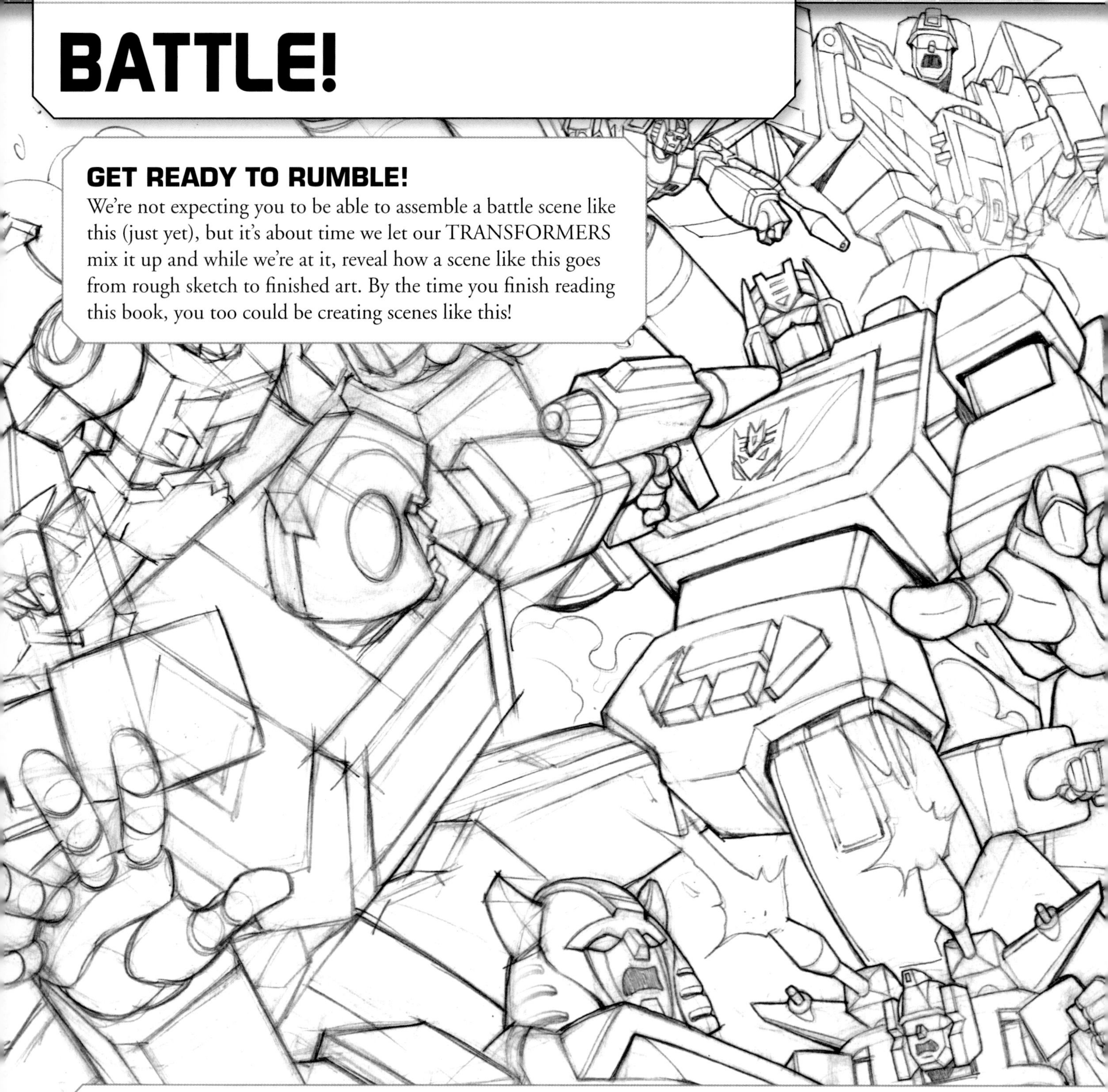

Rough Pencil

First compose the entire scene, roughing it out very loosely on your sketchpad (at a considerably reduced size). Work out where each character will be, what they're doing and their size in relation to one another (taking perspective into account). Then, start in with quite loose pencils, enough to get the very basic figure down on the page. Not too much detail or shading at this stage, as you may well have to erase quite a lot of this preliminary line work.

Finished Pencil

Now go in with a slightly softer pencil lead, tightening up the layout pencils and adding detail and some shading. If you're going to be inking your own pencils, you can leave a lot of the heavy shading out at this stage and introduce it at the next stage (or even at the color stage). Erase any perspective lines or irrelevant layout pencils and add in any background detail or effects (like smoke, impact/motion lines, muzzle flashes, or explosions).

Inked Artwork

Next embellish the pencil lines with ink. Pens, brushes, or markers will enhance and further define the pencil art, as well as adding delineation between the tightly packed characters. The weight or thickness of line used on one character can help to separate foreground and background characters. The inker also adds texture, solid blacks, and shading. For more information see pages 76–81.

Final Color

Though some color artists do still prefer to use paint and brush, increasingly these days colored art is created digitally, on the computer. A wide range of extra options are available to the digital colorist at the touch of a key, such as airbrush effects, flares, and fades. The digital process also allows greater flexibility in terms of color corrections. In the above artwork, the sky is rendered entirely as a computer effect and some shading has been introduced digitally.

OPTIMUS PRIME

Although he is one of the most instantly recognizable TRANSFORMER characters, Optimus Prime's visual appearance has been the subject of much artistic interpretation, not to mention radical reimagination over the course of the last 20 plus years. From Bill Sienkiewicz's original stylised rendering on the cover of Marvel Comics' TRANSFORMERS #1 (1984) to Pat Lee's broad, manga-styled incarnation (2002) Optimus Prime has continually challenged artists to create the *definitive* version.

TRANSFORMERS #1 [2002]

After some years' absence, Optimus Prime returned with a vengeance courtesy of Dreamwave Studios. Their dramatic "house" art style was a big hit and issue #1 topped the Diamond Top 100 sales chart. (Cover art by Pat Lee)

CHARACTER HISTORY

Once a lowly archivist on Cybertron, Optimus Prime had no idea of his mighty destiny, not until the day he was chosen—by the sacred Matrix of Leadership—to lead the heroic Autobots in the struggle against the evil Decepticons and, one day, reunite the warring factions. Prime stood tall and resolute against Megatron's quest for ultimate power during the latter stages of the civil war on Cybertron, and—during a battle aboard the Autobots' giant spacecraft, *The Ark*—made the ultimate sacrifice. Rather than let Megatron's raiding party possess the craft and its awesome firepower, he set the vessel to crash-land on a nearby planet. But, millions of years later, the deactivated Autobots and Decepticons awoke to continue their battle… on Earth!

CYBERTRONIAN FORM

On Cybertron, Optimus Prime's robot and vehicle modes were quite different to those he eventually adopted on Earth. Artist Don Figueroa had to retro-design Optimus Prime, stripping away the more overtly Earthen elements.

TIPS

Optimus Prime is the leader of the good guys and and he should always be portrayed as an heroic, charismatic, calm, and competent character. The body language should reflect this. Unless absolutely necessary, it is preferable not to use aggressive gestures or poses.

Guido Guidi

ROUGH PENCIL DRAWING

First, let's get Prime into an action pose. Don't worry so much about detail. Instead, concentrate on proportion and composition. Start with a loose stick figure, then build in the main human joints before the robot armature.

ROUGH PENCIL DRAWING

First, let's get Prime into an action pose. Don't worry so much about detail. Instead, concentrate on proportion and composition. Start with a loose stick figure, then build in the main human joints before the robot armature.

FINAL PENCIL DRAWING

Next, start in with the fine detail and shading, adding in Prime's hand-held blaster weapon, antennae and (shoulder) exhaust pipes. Remember, Prime's upper torso is basically the front section of the truck, so draw in the shape of a windscreen and work outwards from there.

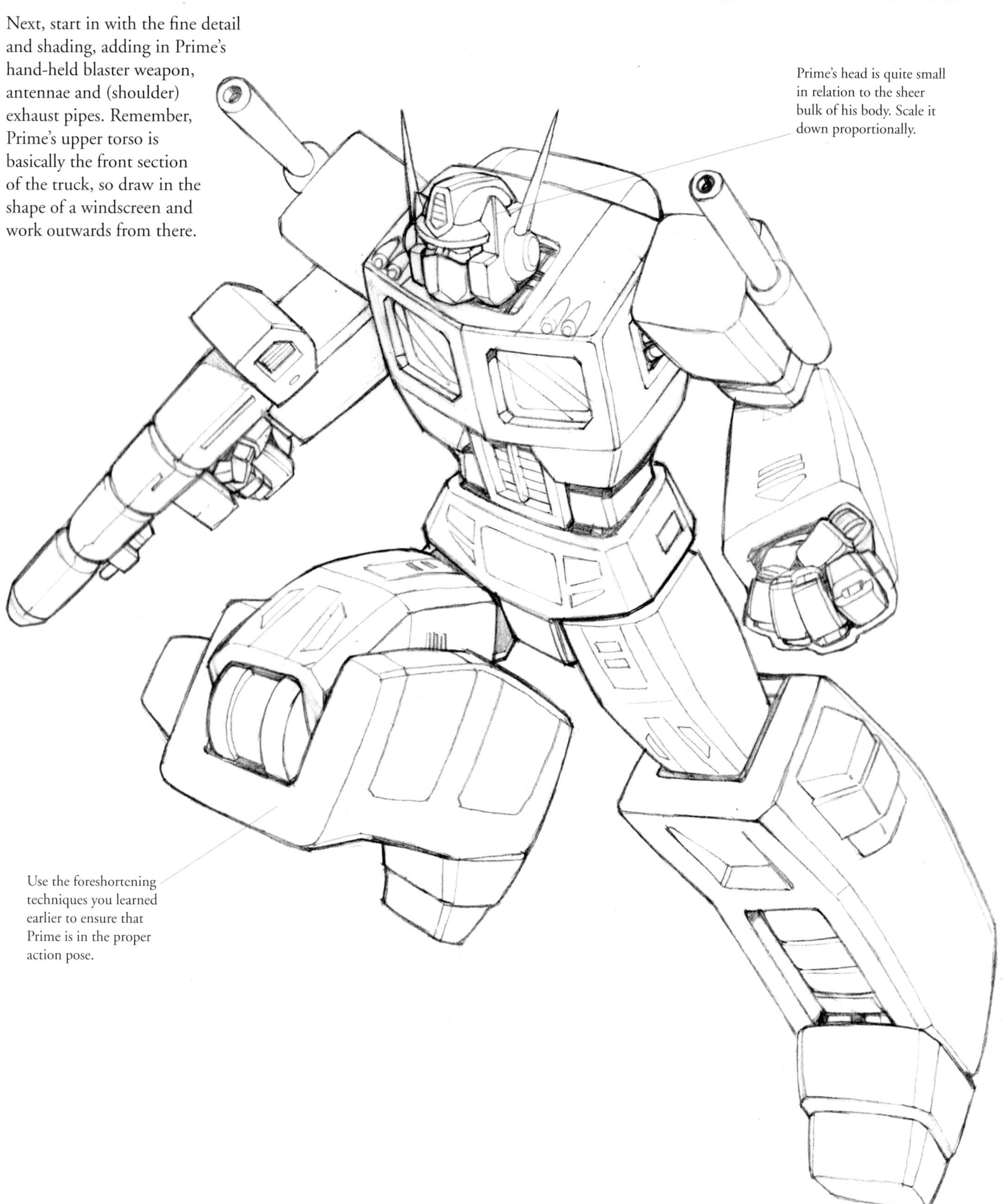

Prime's head is quite small in relation to the sheer bulk of his body. Scale it down proportionally.

Use the foreshortening techniques you learned earlier to ensure that Prime is in the proper action pose.

DETAILS

WEAPONRY

Optimus Prime carries a powerful, long-barreled laser cannon rifle, which—aided by his amazing visual ability—can target and bring down a Decepticon jet at a distance of up to 30 miles (48 kilometers). His right hand is removable, and can be replaced by a solid light battleaxe.

Optimus Prime prepares to battle Megatron atop the Sherman Dam.

THE MATRIX

Housed inside Optimus Prime's specially constructed chest cavity is the Autobot Matrix of Leadership (or Creation Matrix). Each guardian of the Matrix is transformed and sustained by its incredible, regenerative powers (which stem from the all-powerful being known as Primus).

TRANSFORMATION

The Ark's computer, Teletran-1, reconfigured Optimus Prime on his reawakening on Earth. Now in a local disguise, Prime had several separate (but interlinked) components: a trailer, which could open up into an advanced command deck and a remote-controlled reconnaissance unit called Roller. Prime himself transforms into the (front) cab section of the truck/trailer combo.

Optimus Prime: full transformation. From robot mode to truck mode in four stages.

FINAL INKED DRAWING

Use strong bold line work to emphasize the foreground areas of the figure. Heavy black shaded areas will knock the foreshortened (propeling) leg further into the background and help thrust the main torso at us. Well done—you've personally immortalized Optimus Prime on the page!

Be careful when inking that areas of fine detail don't mesh or bleed together.

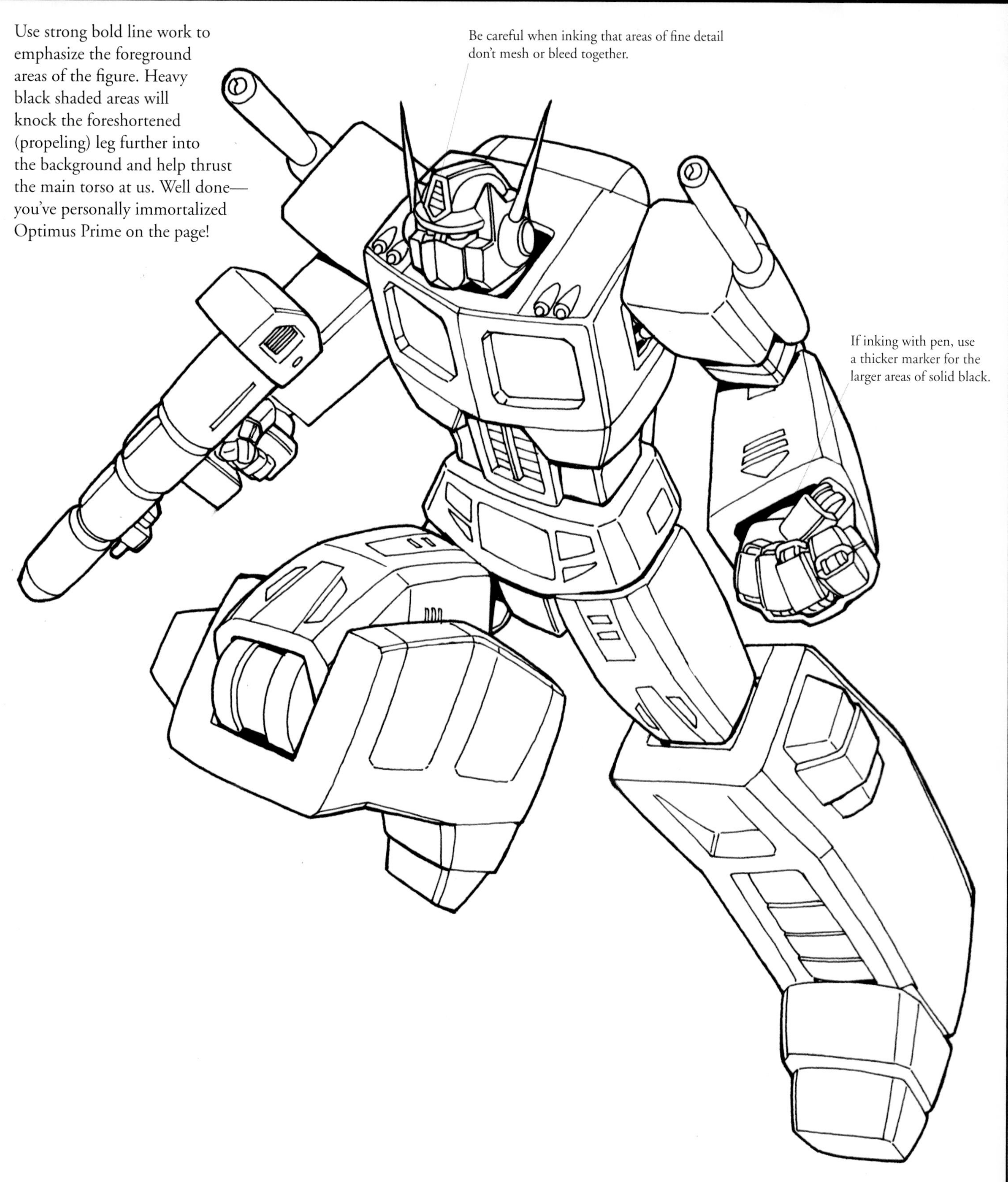

If inking with pen, use a thicker marker for the larger areas of solid black.

HEADS

ABOUT FACE

While some TRANSFORMERS have defined facial features, more often that not an artist will have to make the most of very little. Many characters have visors or faceplates that obscure the lower half (or so) of the face entirely, while others bear almost no resemblance to a human face at all.

Hard Lines

In the case of a robotic character like Galvatron, pictured, you can utilize a basic human face and adapt it. The main difference is that where there are normally soft curves and textures, here there are just hard lines and sharp angles. There's also no hair or eyebrows, no ears, or pupils in the eyes.

STEP-BY-STEP

Before we get onto faces (and heads) that don't conform, let's look at the basics of drawing a head.

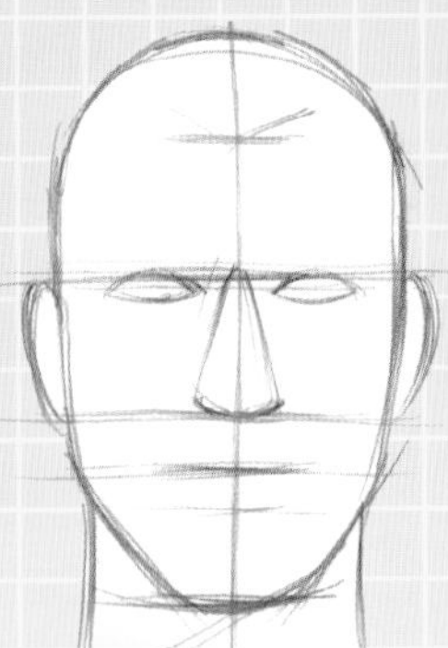

1) Start with an oval shape, like an upside down egg, and draw a vertical line down the middle. Next, sketch in three vertical lines.

2) Use the top vertical line for the eyes, the next for the nose, and the third for the mouth. Add in the detail, plus the ears and hairline.

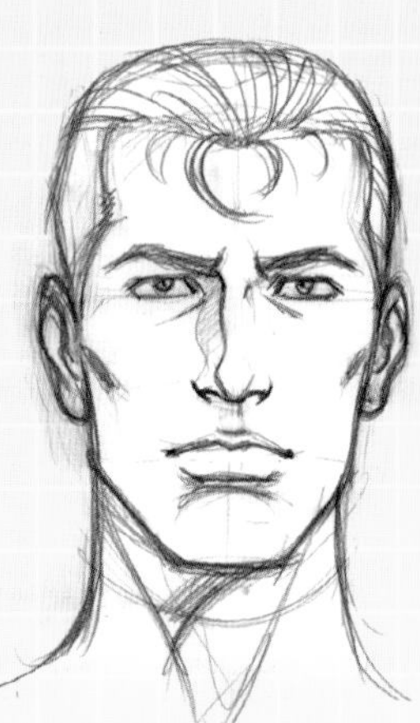

3) Fully render the face, adding detail and shading to the eyes, ears, nose, and mouth and texture to the hair.

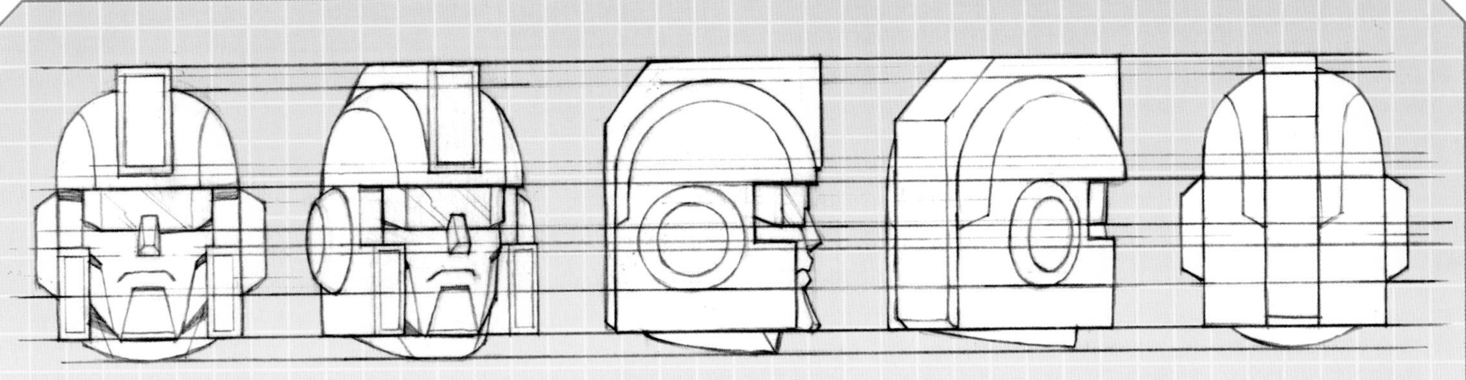

Planes of the Face

A good artist should always know how his character looks from any given angle or viewpoint. The best preparation for this is to sketch out a quick turnaround guide: a series of heads (all in the same exact proportions) viewed through a complete 360-degree rotation. To make your page composition as interesting as possible, select a variety of different angles, especially in static scenes.

VARIATIONS

Pictured here are a number of different shapes of robotic heads. Brawn (top left) has a distinctive dome-shaped head, while Shockwave (top centre) has just a single eye. Bruticus (top right) and Wheeljack (bottom left) feature visor variations, while Starscream (bottom right) has a boxy, rectangular head.

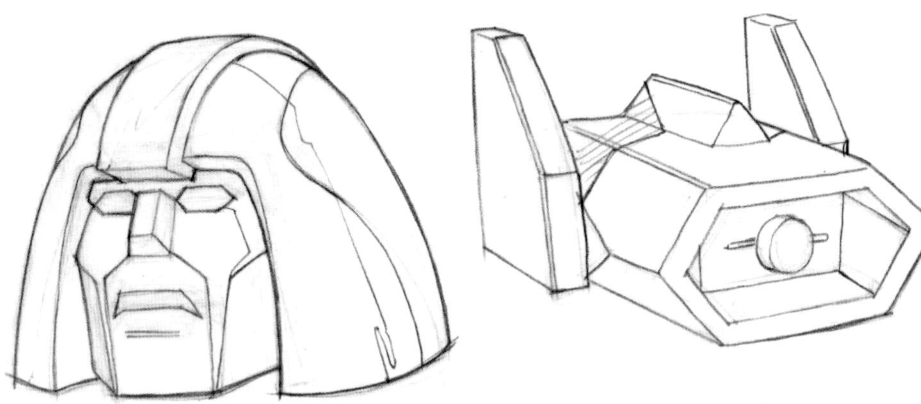

YOUR TURN

Because, often, a character (such as Optimus Prime) has little in the way of facial features to work with, practice working expression into (and around) the eyes. Draw a series of narrow rectangles and try for as broad a range of basic emotions (anger, suspicion, surprise) as possible. Body language is also very important here.

HANDS

A HELPING HAND

When drawing robotic characters that have few facial features, it's worth noting that hands can be expressive too. For example, a clenched fist denotes anger or stoic determination, while an open hand suggests shock or peaceful overtures.

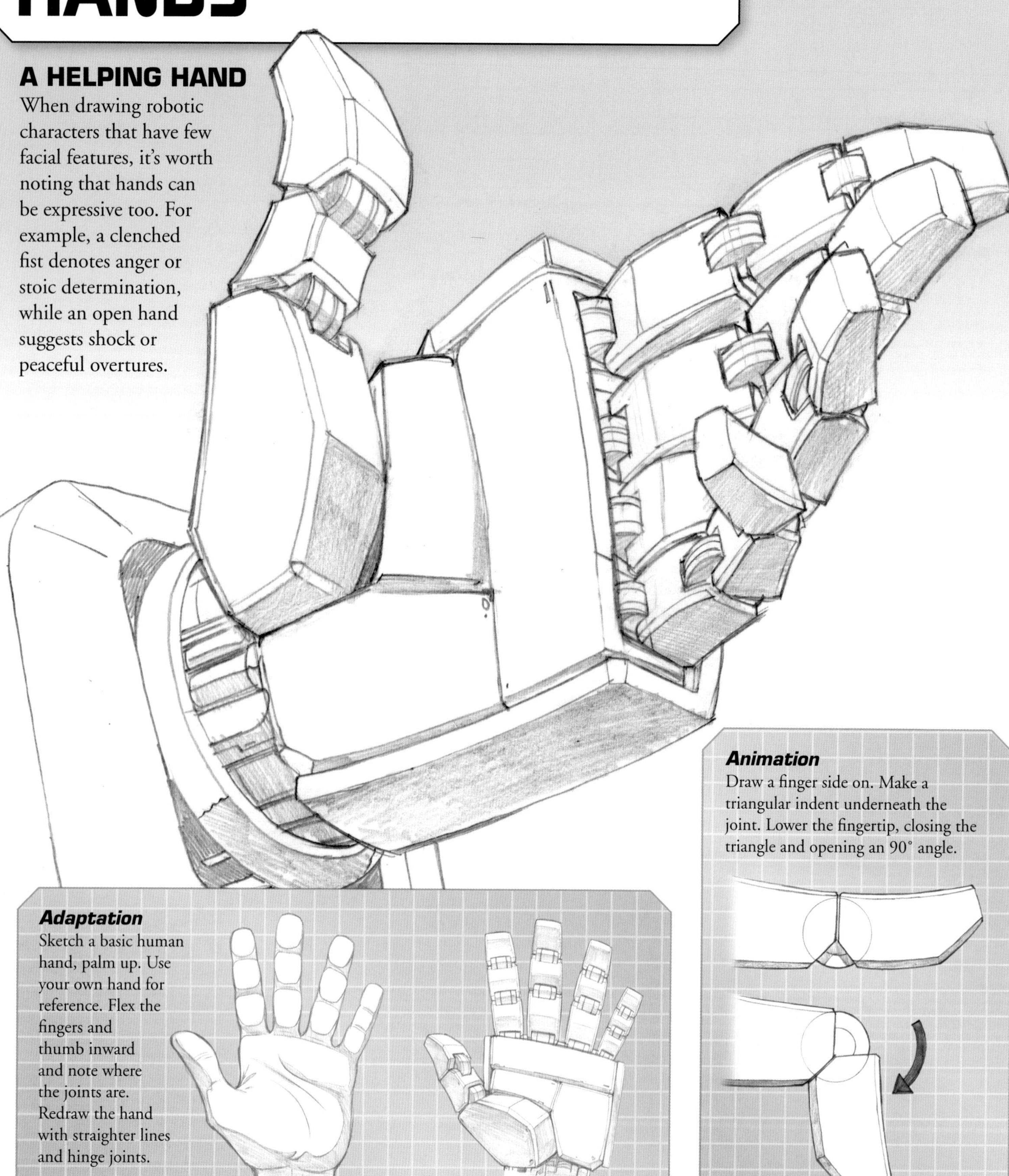

Animation

Draw a finger side on. Make a triangular indent underneath the joint. Lower the fingertip, closing the triangle and opening an 90° angle.

Adaptation

Sketch a basic human hand, palm up. Use your own hand for reference. Flex the fingers and thumb inward and note where the joints are. Redraw the hand with straighter lines and hinge joints.

Fists

Study your own hand, but this time clenched into a fist. Look at it from a variety of different angles and draw it first as a human fist then as robotic one.

Front view: see how the fingers bend in to the palm and the thumb wraps around them.

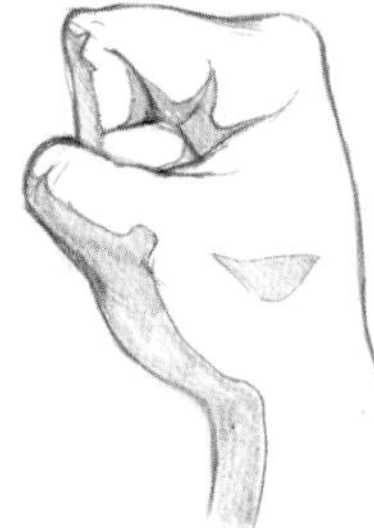

Side view: see how the index finger is bent inwards, allowing the thumb to grip underneath.

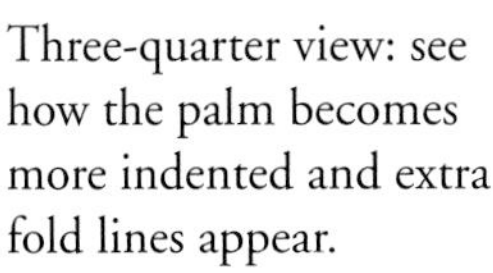

Three-quarter view: see how the palm becomes more indented and extra fold lines appear.

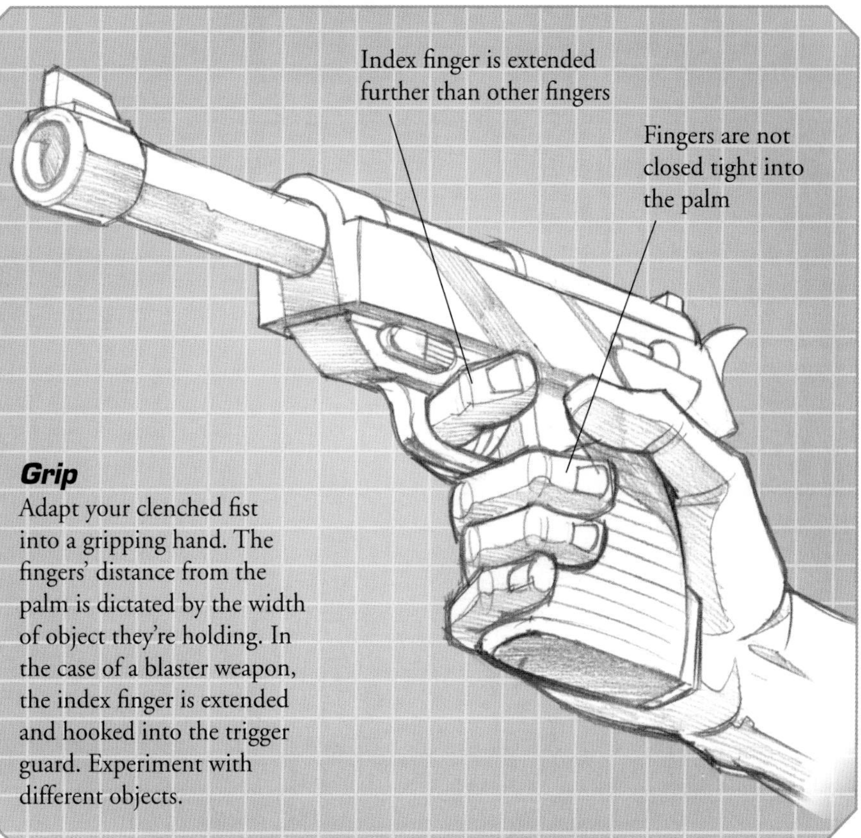
Index finger is extended further than other fingers
Fingers are not closed tight into the palm

Grip

Adapt your clenched fist into a gripping hand. The fingers' distance from the palm is dictated by the width of object they're holding. In the case of a blaster weapon, the index finger is extended and hooked into the trigger guard. Experiment with different objects.

SKETCHBOOK

Hands are difficult to draw and require lots of practice. Select a variety of different hand positions and gestures and draw these from as many different angles as possible. For example, consider foreshortening in a pointed finger or shadows from a directional light source.

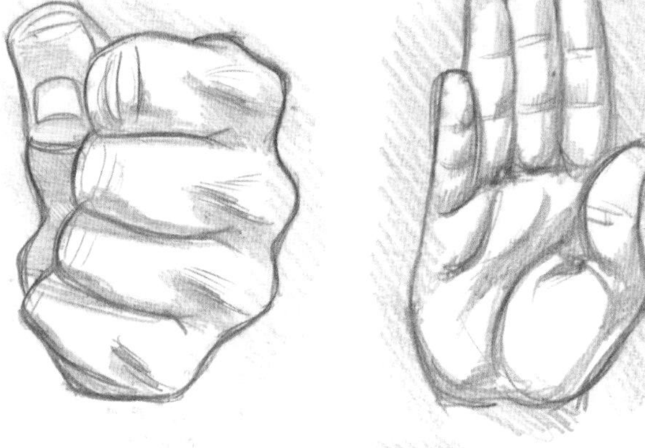

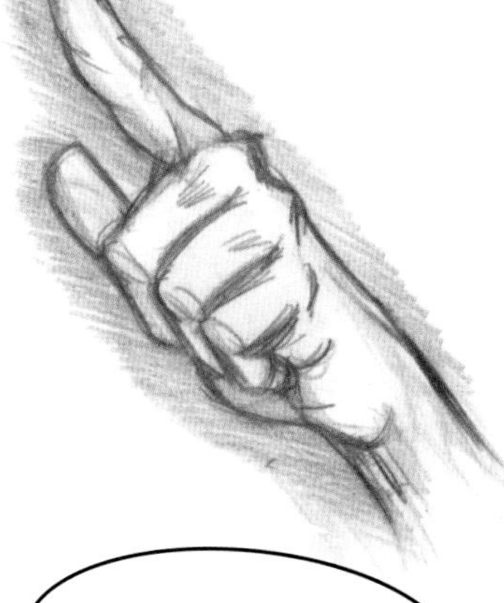

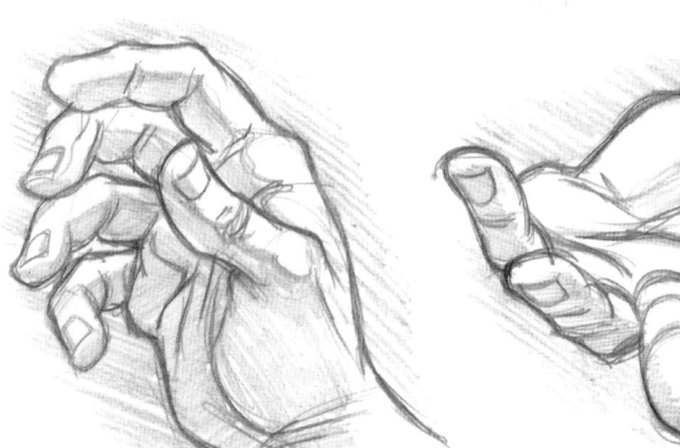

TIPS

Hands are one of the most difficult things to draw correctly, but they are also the easiest thing to find reference for as you have two hands to look at! If you need to draw the drawing hand use a mirror. A digital camera is also handy to have around your drawing table.

E.J. Su

LEGS & FEET

FIRM FOOTING

It's sometimes easy to forget that characters start from the ground up. Every pose, every action shot requires the support—quite literally—of the feet and legs. And whereas TRANSFORMER faces and hands conform, in varying degrees, to human standards, legs and feet tend to be far more unique.

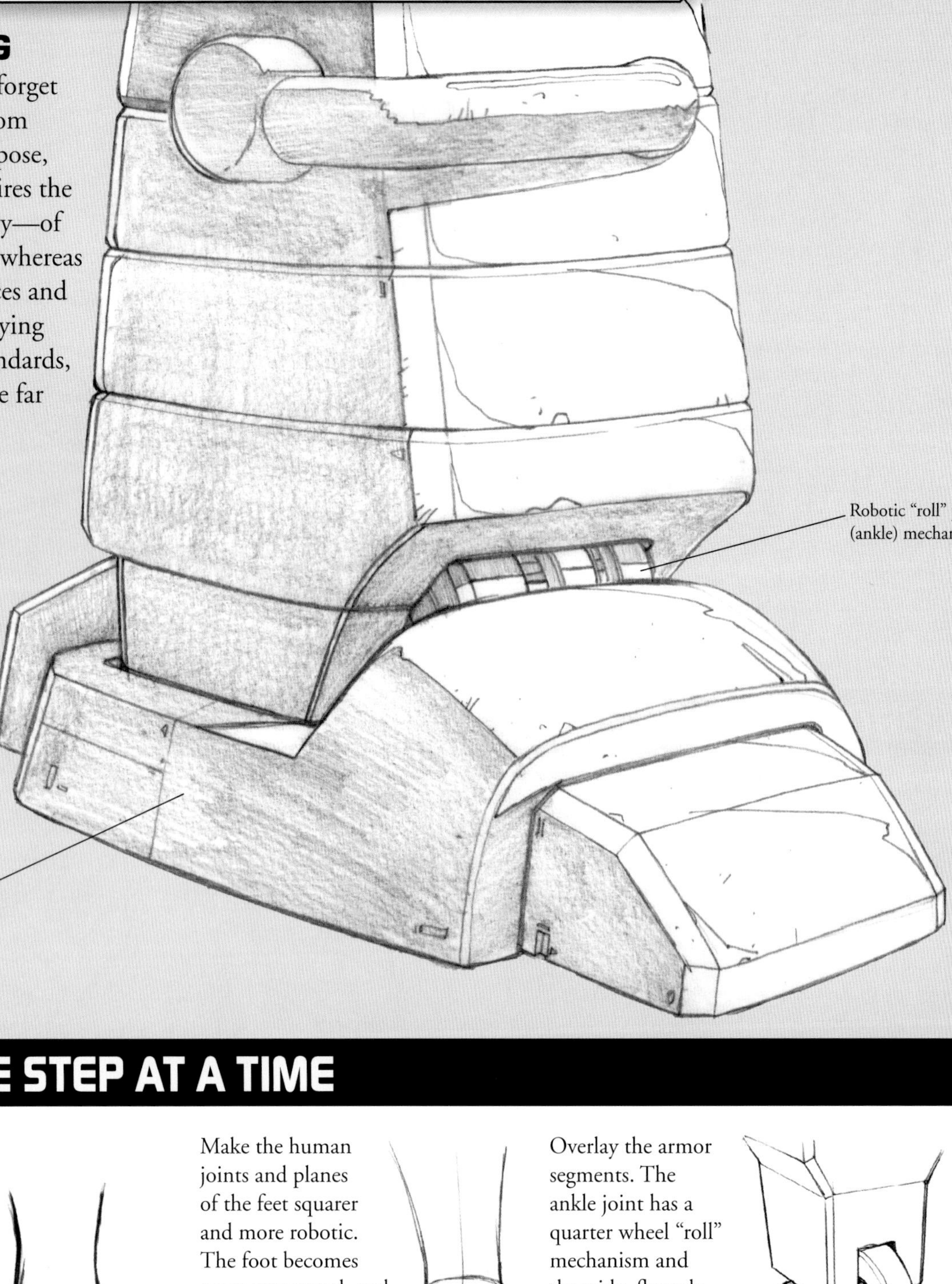

Robotic "roll" joint (ankle) mechanism

Broad based foot for weight distribution

FEET – ONE STEP AT A TIME

Let's start by sketching a regular human foot. At its simplest, it's a cylinder connected to a rounded-off rectangle.

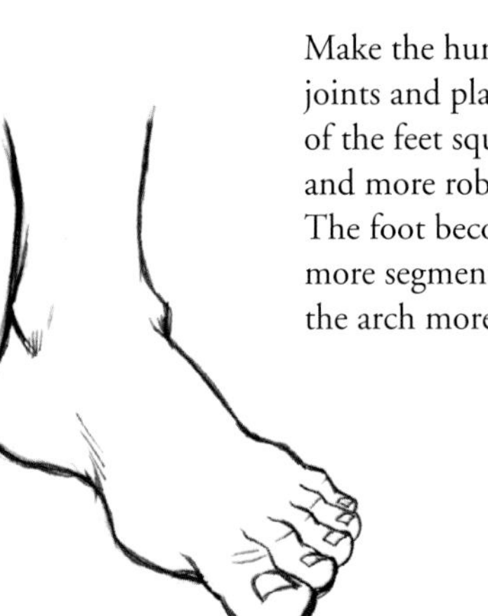

Make the human joints and planes of the feet squarer and more robotic. The foot becomes more segmented, and the arch more raised.

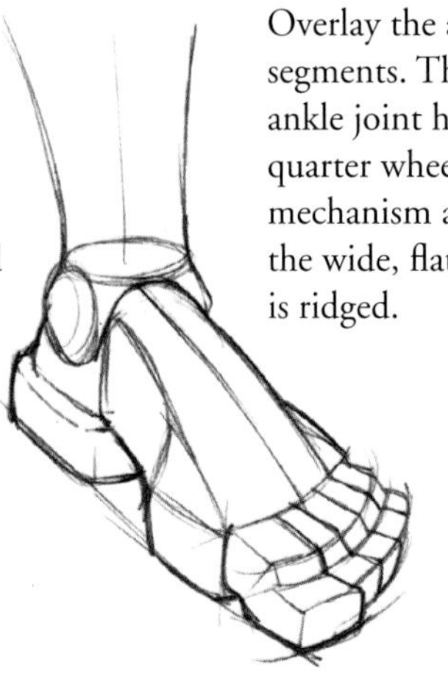

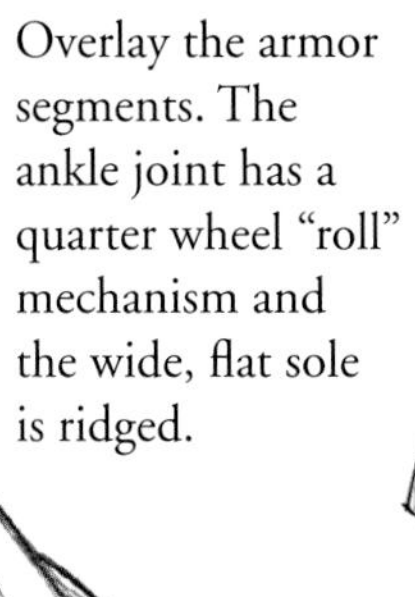

Overlay the armor segments. The ankle joint has a quarter wheel "roll" mechanism and the wide, flat sole is ridged.

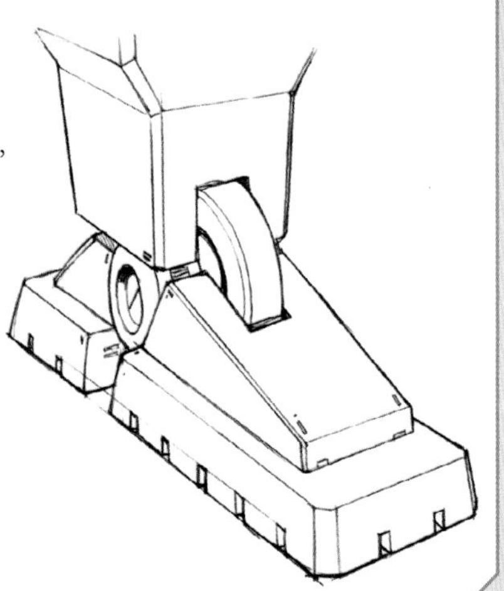

Here are some specific (and differing) examples of TRANSFORMERS' legs and feet, based on actual characters:

STEP-BY-STEP

Galvatron's leg begins with a cylinder, divided at its mid-point. A circle forms the knee guard and a second (overlaid) cylinder forms the lower leg.

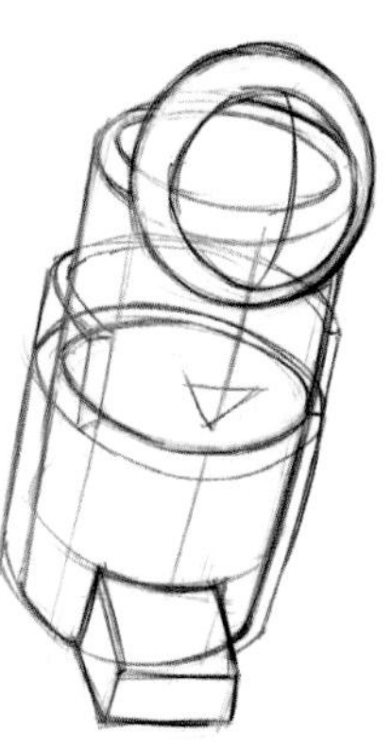

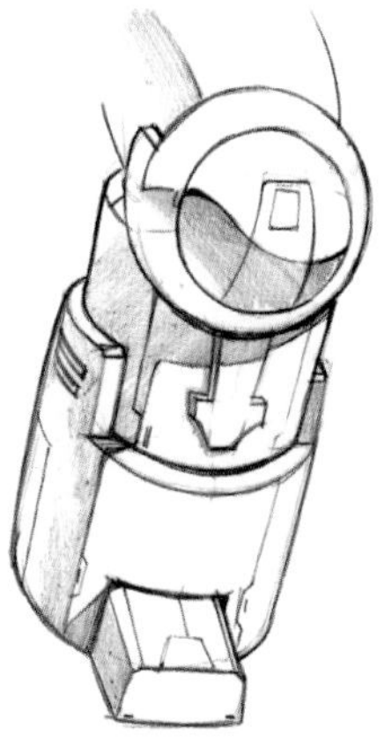

Galvatron

STEP-BY-STEP

Fizzle's leg is formed from two angled cuboids, one inset inside the other. The front section is shaped as the knee and foot, with a tire added to the outer shin.

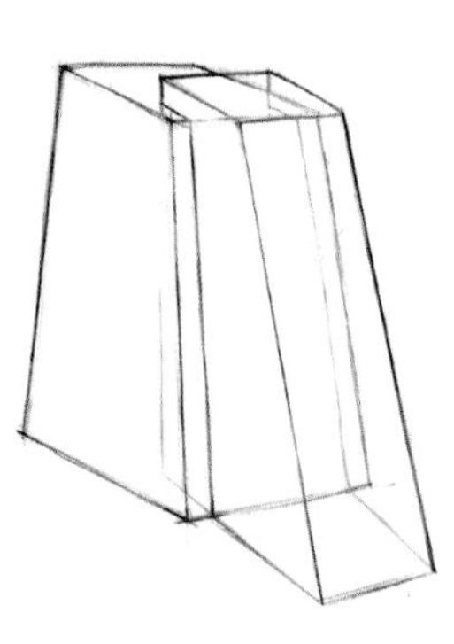

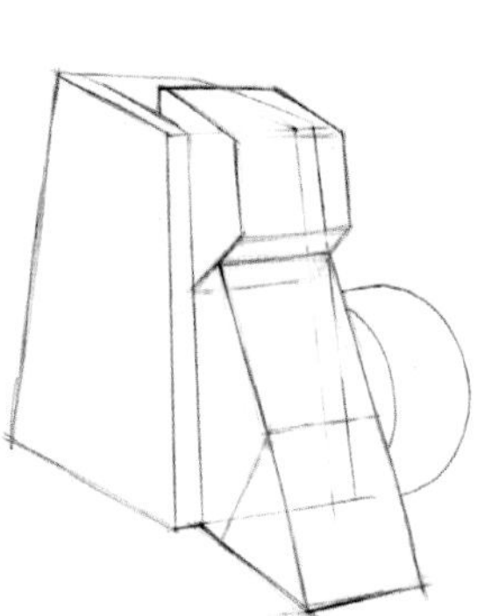

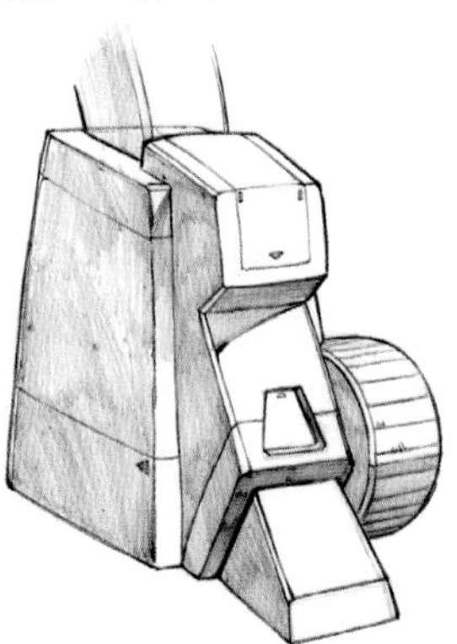

Fizzle

STEP-BY-STEP

Freeway's feet are the two halves of his vehicle mode's bonnet and his heel is the wheel. The knee joint operates on a roll mechanism, whereas the ankle is fixed.

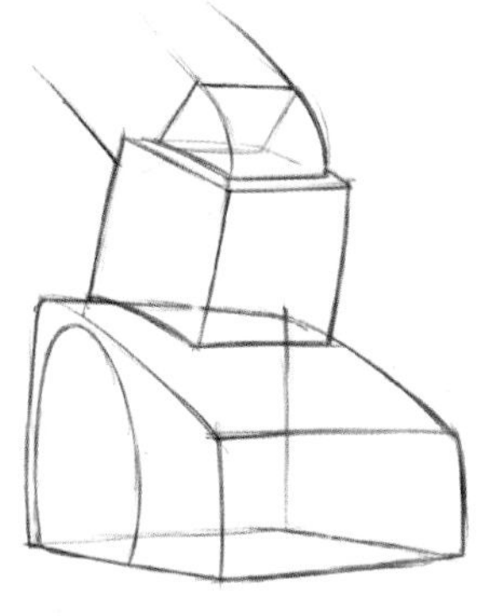

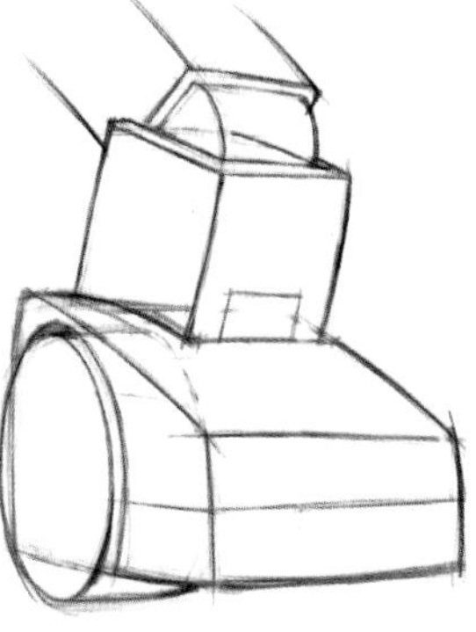

Freeway

DETAILS

UP CLOSE AND PERSONAL

From insignias and battle damage, to vents and tires, TRANSFORMERS come with a wealth of body elements, all of which contribute to their alt. mode or simply add detail. Sometimes it's a purely practical addition, with a specific function, other times it's pure artistic licence, adding unspecified alien tech for extra effect.

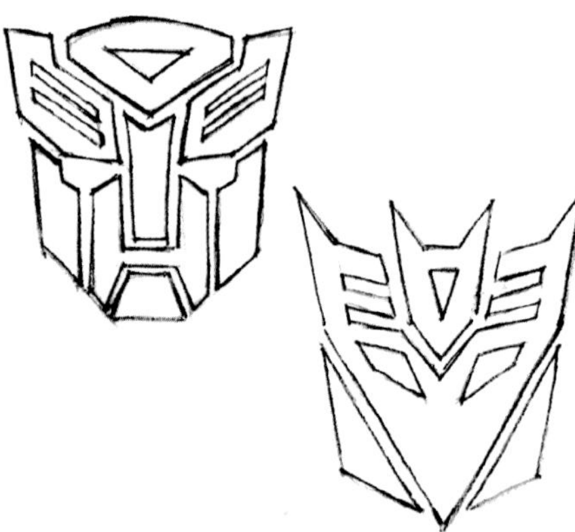

Insignia
The Autobot insignia (left) is based on a vaguely humanoid face, whereas the Decepticon insignia (right) is much more animalistic.

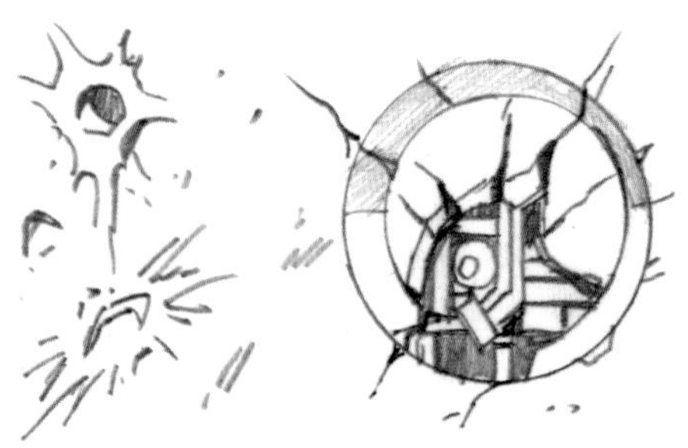

Battle Damage
Realistic and consistent (from one panel to the next) battle damage adds considerably to the overall impact of a character, emphasizing their strength and resilience.

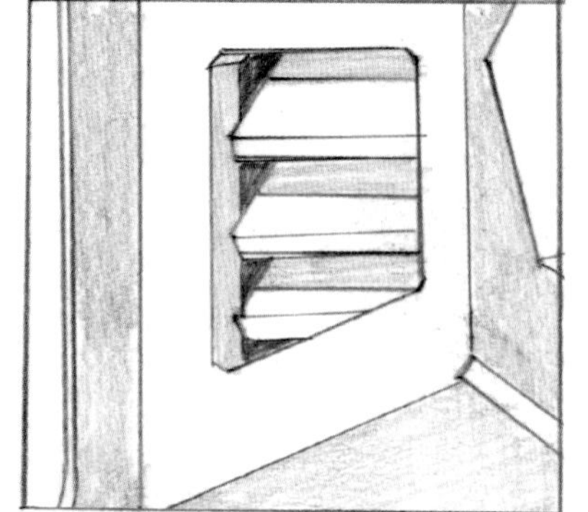

Vents
More decorative than anything, vents do have practical applications. Just cut away a section of armor and add angled strips like those above.

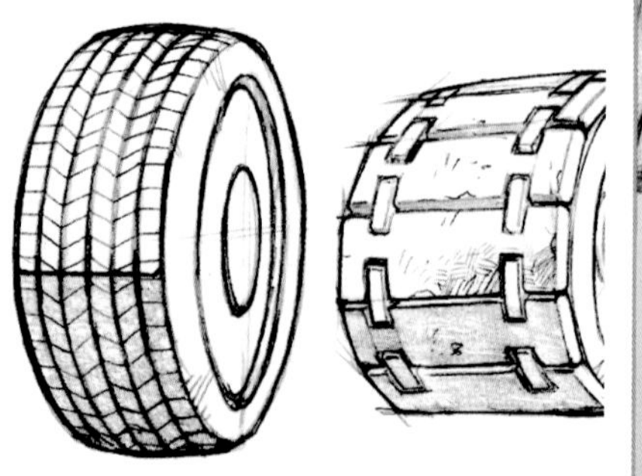

Wheels and Tracks
Whether it's tires or tank tracks, fine detailing (treads, etc) is essential, otherwise they can just look like random body segments or joints.

TIPS

It's important to make details as real and believable as possible. I like to show the knee, elbow, and finger joints and vehicle details like tires and screws too. When a TRANSFORMER is damaged, I draw the inner mechanical and structural parts. Look for reference material on the internet if you are unsure. For insignias and logos, I like to draw them as an extra part of the robot body. So I usually add depth and more details (like screws) on them.

Marcelo Matere

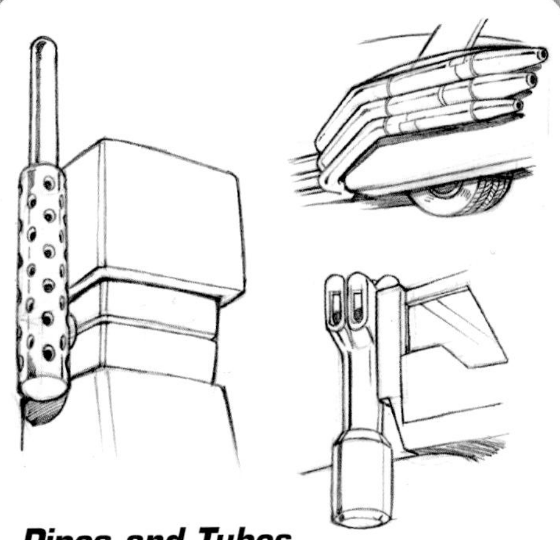

Pipes and Tubes

Often these are specific to the character's type of vehicular alt. mode and so should be used sparingly. Again, fine detailing is important.

Joints

Arm joints tend to be spherical (ball joints) or hinged. Always consider if a recessed space is necessary into which the joint can fit.

SKETCHBOOK

Practice by isolating sections of vehicular and more general alt. modes and familiarize yourself with the mechanics of their (real world) operation. Here are just a few examples…

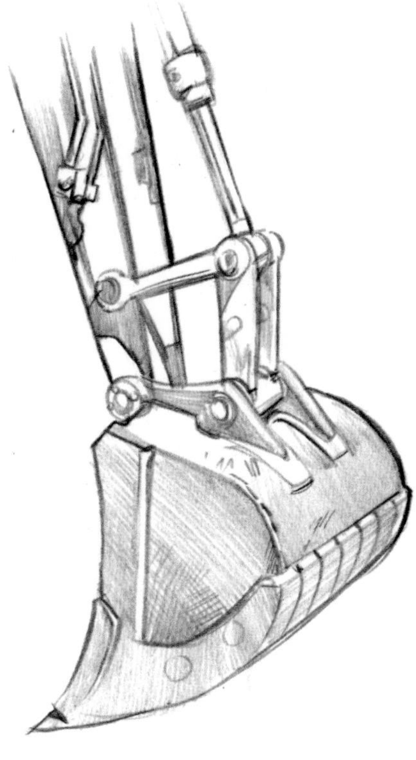

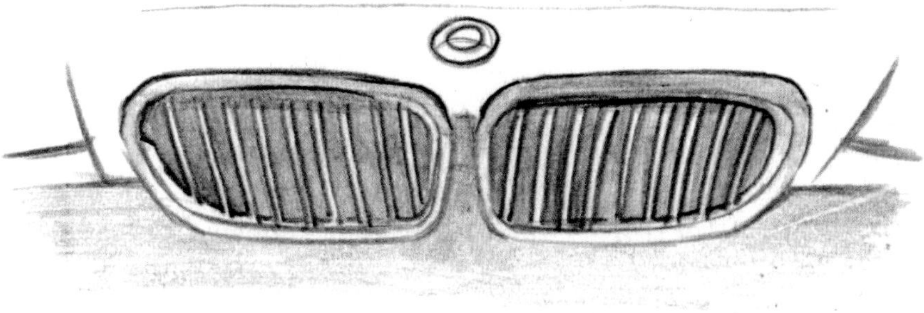

WEAPONS

LOCK AND LOAD!

Every self-respecting giant robot needs a seriously BIG gun. Be it inbuilt, shoulder-mounted or hand-held, in the battle for Cybertron, heavy artillery inevitably comes into play. Alien tech weaponry is pretty much an artistic free for all. There are no hard and fast rules, and the only limitation is your imagination. Here are just a few examples of TRANSFORMERS-friendly weaponry…

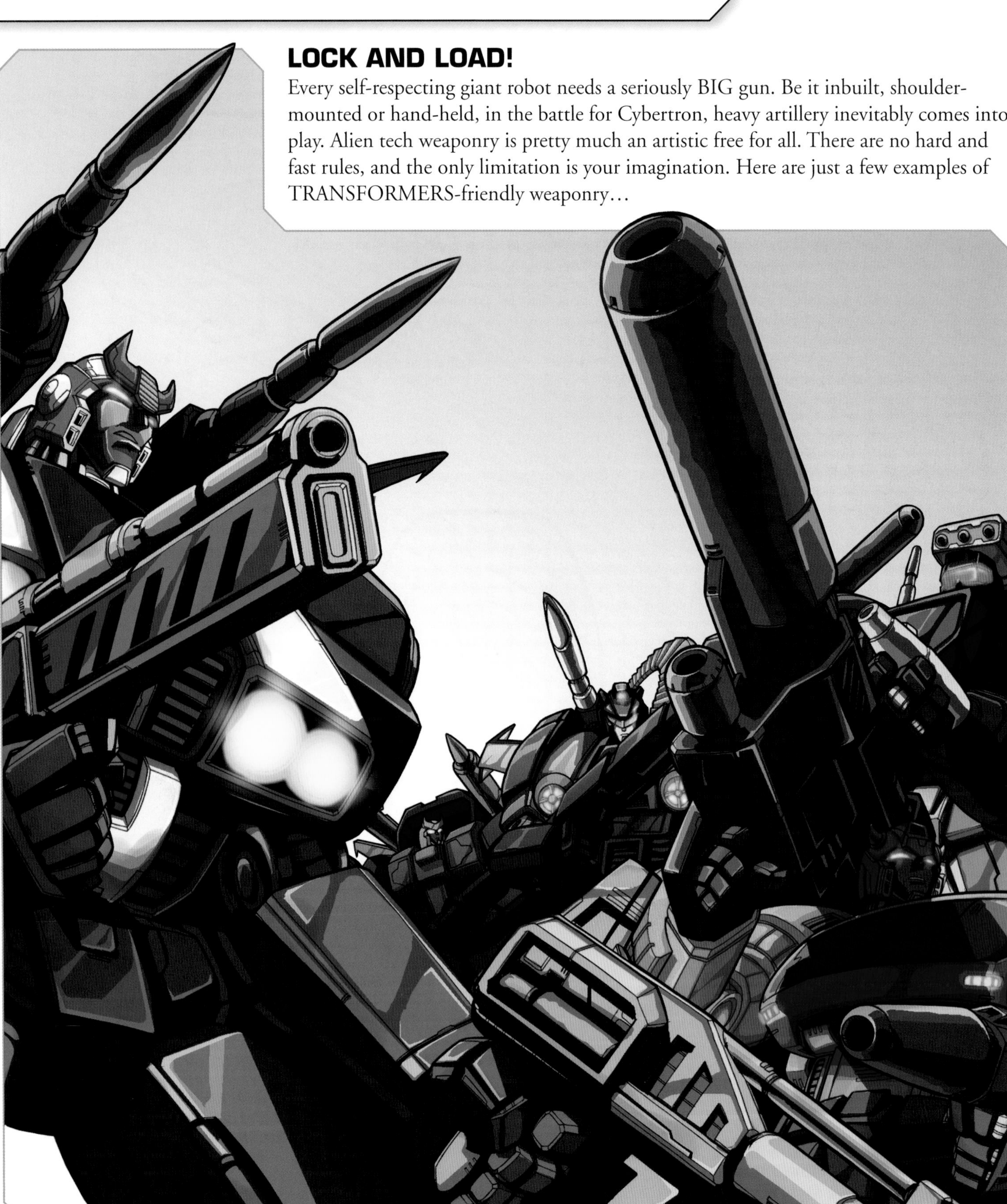

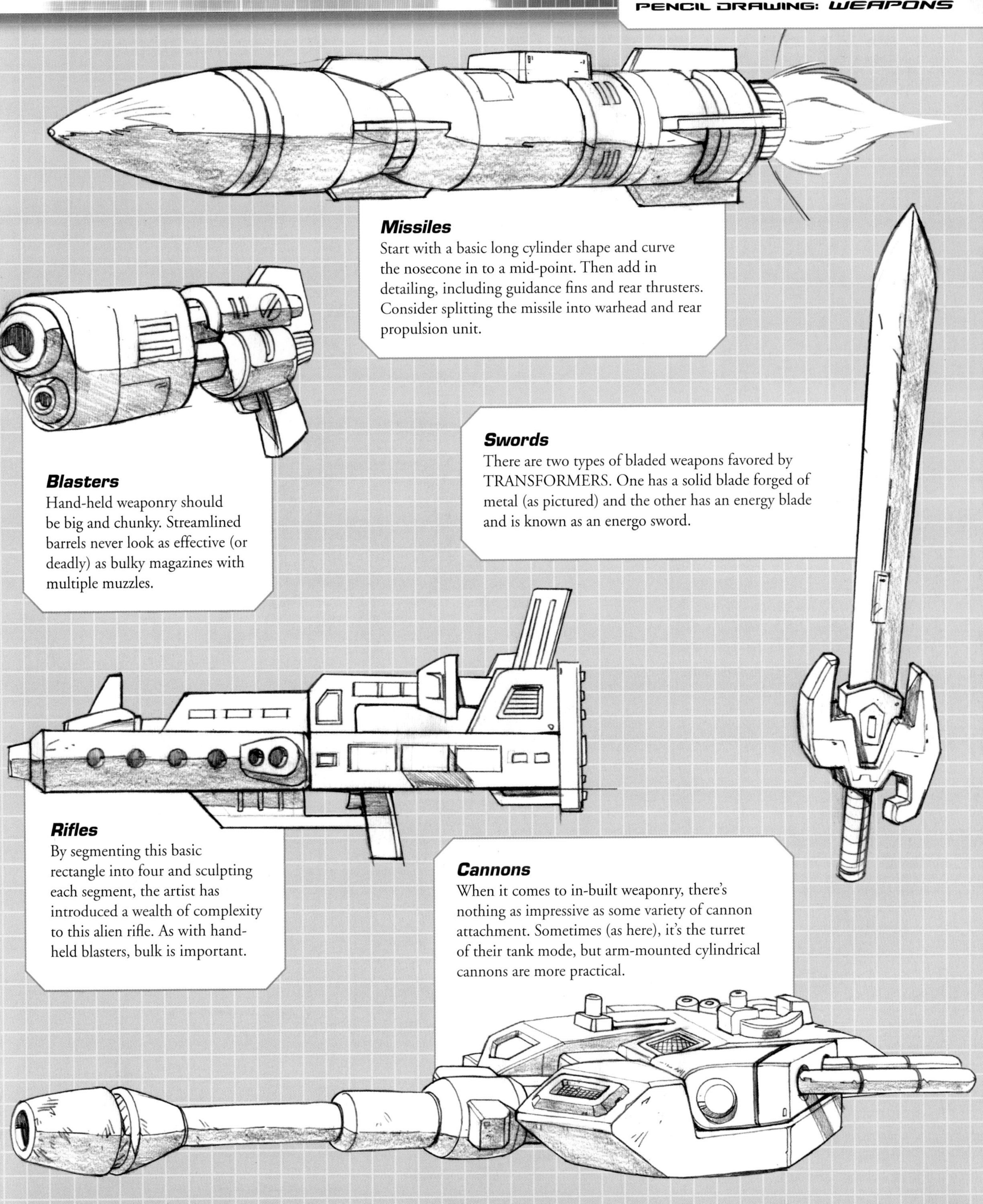

Missiles

Start with a basic long cylinder shape and curve the nosecone in to a mid-point. Then add in detailing, including guidance fins and rear thrusters. Consider splitting the missile into warhead and rear propulsion unit.

Blasters

Hand-held weaponry should be big and chunky. Streamlined barrels never look as effective (or deadly) as bulky magazines with multiple muzzles.

Swords

There are two types of bladed weapons favored by TRANSFORMERS. One has a solid blade forged of metal (as pictured) and the other has an energy blade and is known as an energo sword.

Rifles

By segmenting this basic rectangle into four and sculpting each segment, the artist has introduced a wealth of complexity to this alien rifle. As with hand-held blasters, bulk is important.

Cannons

When it comes to in-built weaponry, there's nothing as impressive as some variety of cannon attachment. Sometimes (as here), it's the turret of their tank mode, but arm-mounted cylindrical cannons are more practical.

GENERATION 1

WHERE IT ALL BEGAN

Back in 1984, Generation 1 (as it has since been dubbed) introduced the founding characters and concepts behind TRANSFORMERS, providing the foundations on which all else has been built.

STEP-BY-STEP

Here's Autobot sub-commander Prowl, from start to finish...

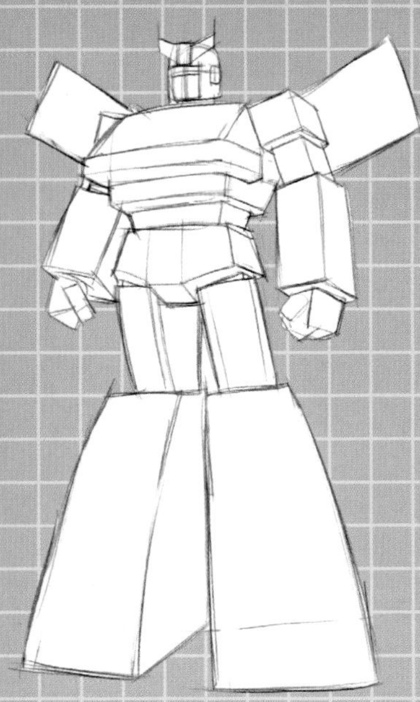

1) Overlay the stick figure with basic shapes to make up the robot body. Don't forget Prowl's distinctive jutting door fins.

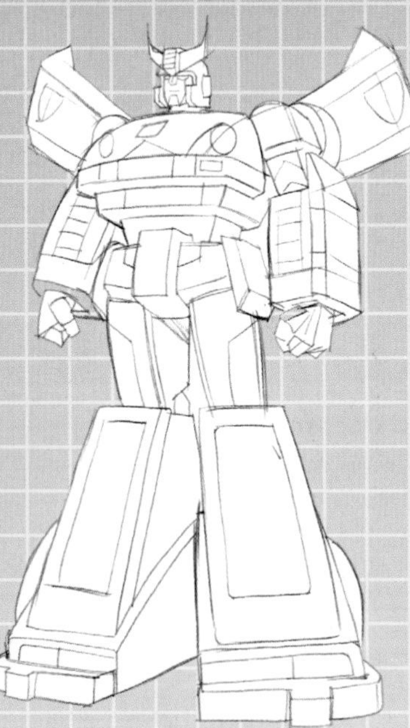

2) Add outline detail and smooth off hard edges. Add triangular tips to Prowl's door fins and clip the lower corner.

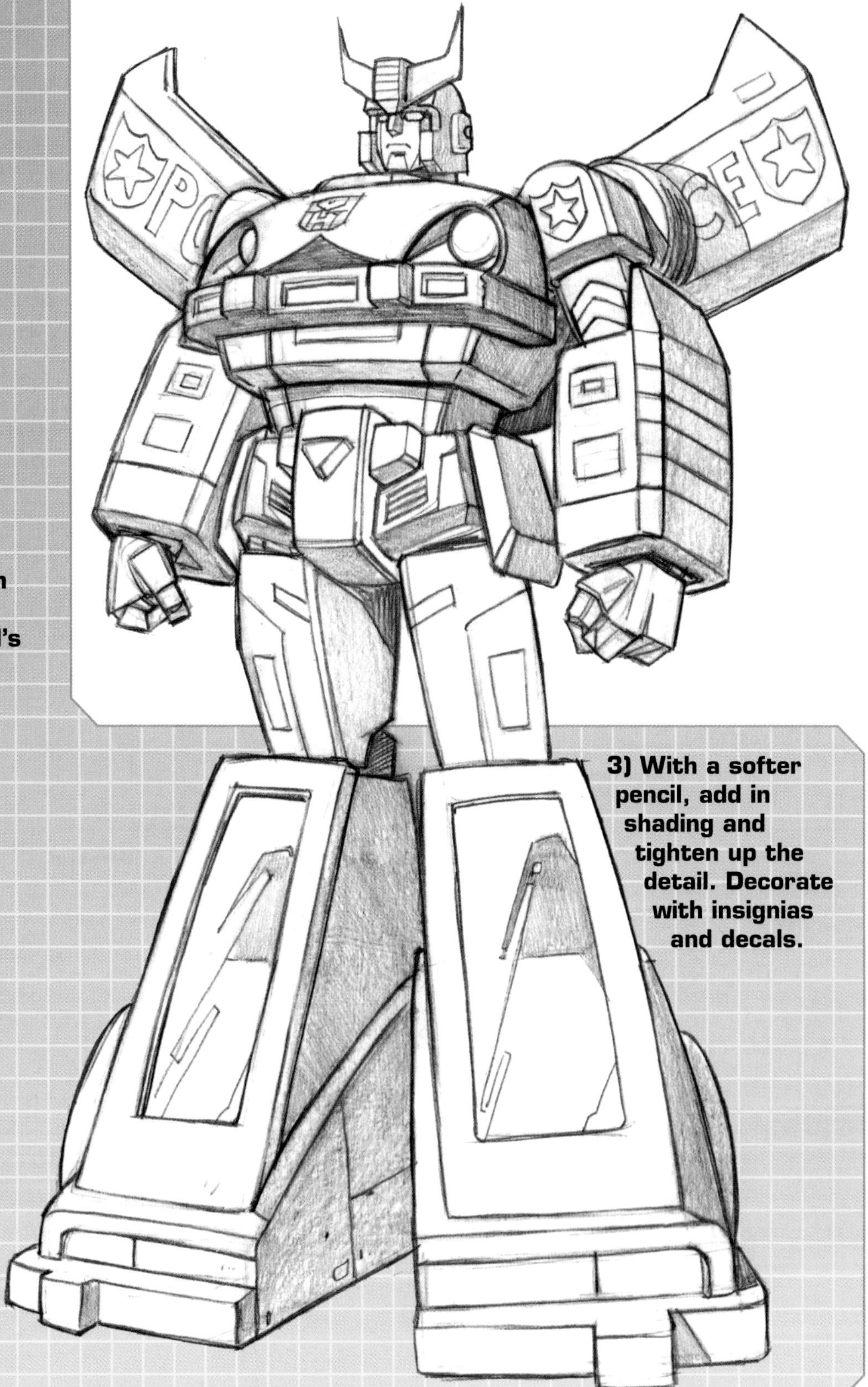

3) With a softer pencil, add in shading and tighten up the detail. Decorate with insignias and decals.

AUTOBOTS

Road Warriors

Early Generation 1 Autobots are almost all vehicular (and ground-based). Until the advent of the likes of Cosmos, Powerglide, and the Aerialbots, only Jetfire could fly in his alt. vehicle mode.

Jazz

Jetfire

Hound

DECEPTICONS

A Mixed Bag

The early Decepticons came in all shapes and forms. From (F15) jets like Starscream, to beasts like Ravage. They, along with Frenzy (who transformed into a cassette) were all part of Soundwave's personal spy network. Soundwave himself transformed into a tape deck.

Ravage

Skyuwarp

Soundwave

DINOBOTS & INSECTICONS

GRIMLOCK

The Dinobots broke the mold of the early Generation 1 characters. Modeled on dinosaurs from Earth's prehistory, their beast modes made them visually distinct from the other Autobots. Dinobot leader, Grimlock, transformed into a Tyrannosaurus Rex lookalike.

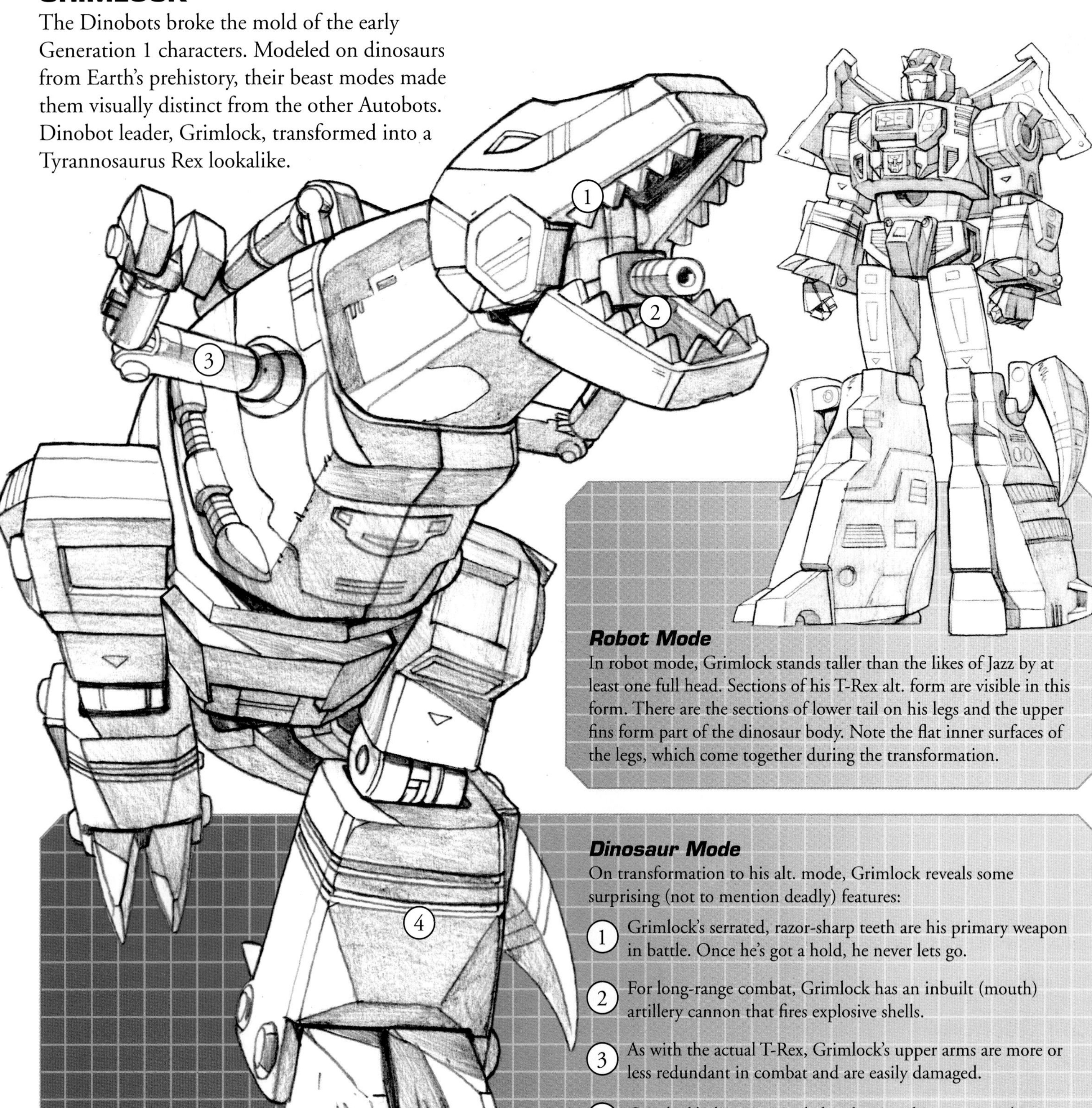

Robot Mode

In robot mode, Grimlock stands taller than the likes of Jazz by at least one full head. Sections of his T-Rex alt. form are visible in this form. There are the sections of lower tail on his legs and the upper fins form part of the dinosaur body. Note the flat inner surfaces of the legs, which come together during the transformation.

Dinosaur Mode

On transformation to his alt. mode, Grimlock reveals some surprising (not to mention deadly) features:

1. Grimlock's serrated, razor-sharp teeth are his primary weapon in battle. Once he's got a hold, he never lets go.
2. For long-range combat, Grimlock has an inbuilt (mouth) artillery cannon that fires explosive shells.
3. As with the actual T-Rex, Grimlock's upper arms are more or less redundant in combat and are easily damaged.
4. Grimlock's dinosaur mode legs become his arms in robot mode, his hands extending from recessed compartments.

Shrapnel

Just as the Autobots had the Dinobots, the Decepticons had the Insecticons, a loathsome trio of acid secreting individuals. Shrapnel (pictured here) generated devastating bolts of electrical energy. His (stag beetle-like) alt. mode is a highly complex design.

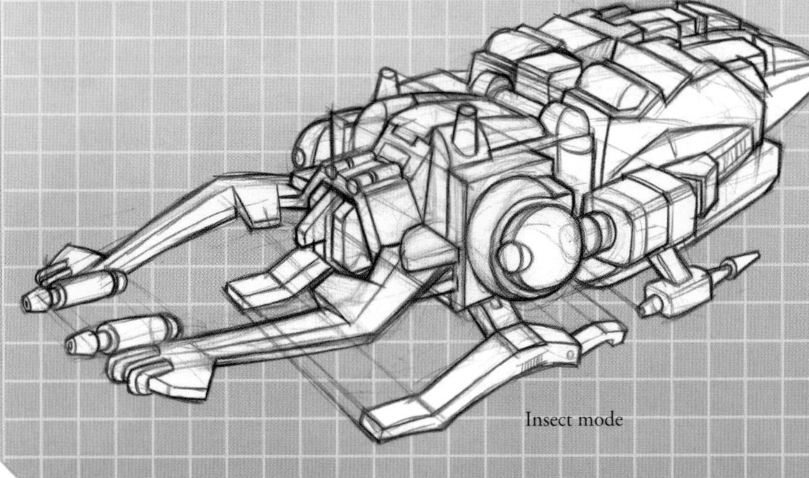

Insect mode

Robot mode

Roll Call

The trio of Insecticons included Kickback (a grasshopper) and Bombshell (a rhinoceros beetle), while the Dinobot quintet had Slag (Triceratops), Swoop (Pterandon), Sludge (Brontosaurus), and Snarl (Stegosaurus).

Kickback

Bombshell

When drawing animal TRANSFORMERS like the Dinobots and Insecticons, check out how real insects look and move and get reference on actual dinosaurs. Then apply what you've learned to your drawings; make the Insecticons creepy and scary, and the Dinobots look huge and powerful, just like the real thing!

Nick Roche

Slag

Swoop

Sludge

Snarl

COMBINERS

THE CONSTRUCTICONS

The first group of combining TRANSFORMERS to hit the scene were the Constructicons, a Decepticon-affiliated group of engineers and scientists. The six Constructicons merged through a complex series of transformations and interlocking maneuvers into Devastator.

Long Haul

Scrapper

Hook

Scavenger

Bonecrusher

Mixmaster

STEP-BY-STEP

When drawing Devastator, first identify which individual robot becomes what...

1) Assemble the suitably transformed Constructicons: Hook (head), Long Haul (torso), Bonecrusher (left arm), Scavenger (right arm), Mixmaster (left leg) and Scrapper (right leg).

2) Now sketch in the detail of the overall (combined) super-robot, defining the shapes and accessories of the individuals and adding in the chest (connector) segment.

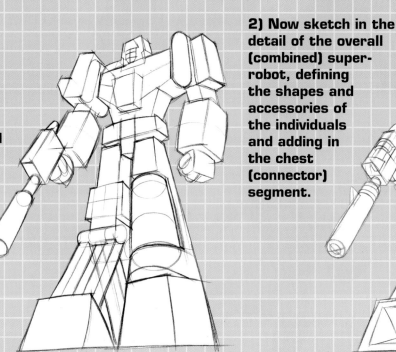

3) Finally, add the fine detail and shading, plus Decepticon insignia and open out any inset or hollow areas. Devastator stands around 30 heads tall.

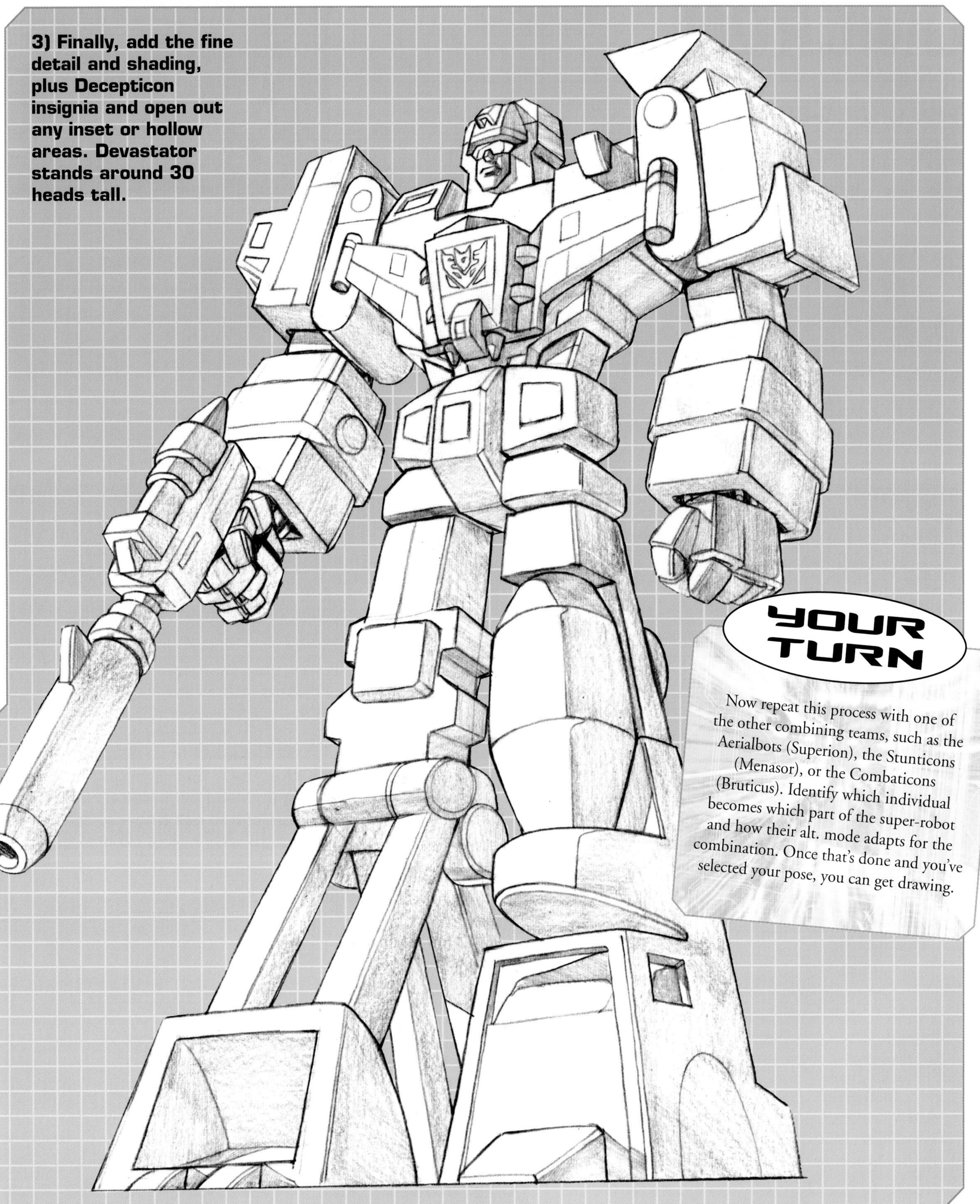

YOUR TURN

Now repeat this process with one of the other combining teams, such as the Aerialbots (Superion), the Stunticons (Menasor), or the Combaticons (Bruticus). Identify which individual becomes which part of the super-robot and how their alt. mode adapts for the combination. Once that's done and you've selected your pose, you can get drawing.

UNICRON

THE CHAOS-BRINGER

They don't come any bigger than Unicron, the ultimate enemy of the TRANSFORMERS (as a whole). Unicron doesn't so much want to conquer Cybertron… as eat it! In his planetary mode, Unicron can shatter whole worlds with his pincers and then consume them. Cybertron is always on the menu.

Unicron made his debut in the 1985 animated *TRANSFORMERS: The Movie*. He was voiced by the late Orson Welles.

STEP-BY-STEP

Though enormous (in relation to other TRANSFORMERS), drawing Unicron is just like drawing any other robot. The same basic rules apply.

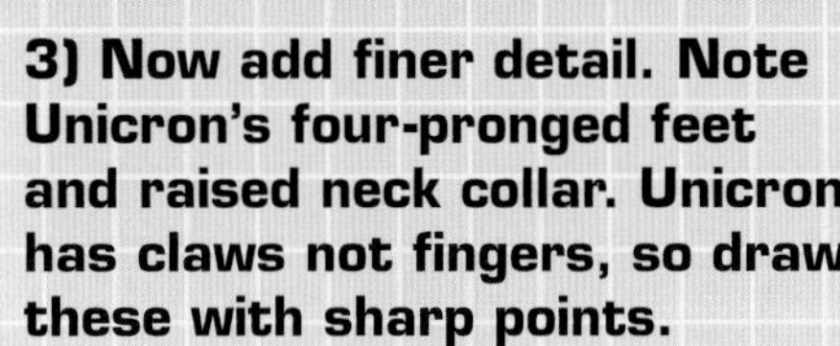

1) First, select your pose. Being of giant size, Unicron tends to loom over other characters. A slightly shoulders-hunched position is most effective here.

2) Once the basic box-shapes have been added (on the body), sketch in the "wings" which are formed from the outer sensor ring (in planet mode).

3) Now add finer detail. Note Unicron's four-pronged feet and raised neck collar. Unicron has claws not fingers, so draw these with sharp points.

Infinite Evil

Created at the dawn of time, Unicron is evil personified, more a force of nature than an actual living entity. He exists to consume and ravage whole worlds, entire systems, the very fabric of space and time itself, and he is very, very hard to kill. Because he exists in multiple realities and assorted time zones (simultaneously), the destruction of one physical form is little more than an inconvenience. The only thing Unicron truly fears, the only thing that can destroy him utterly, is the living essence of Primus, lord of light (a fraction of which is contained within the Autobots' sacred Matrix of Leadership).

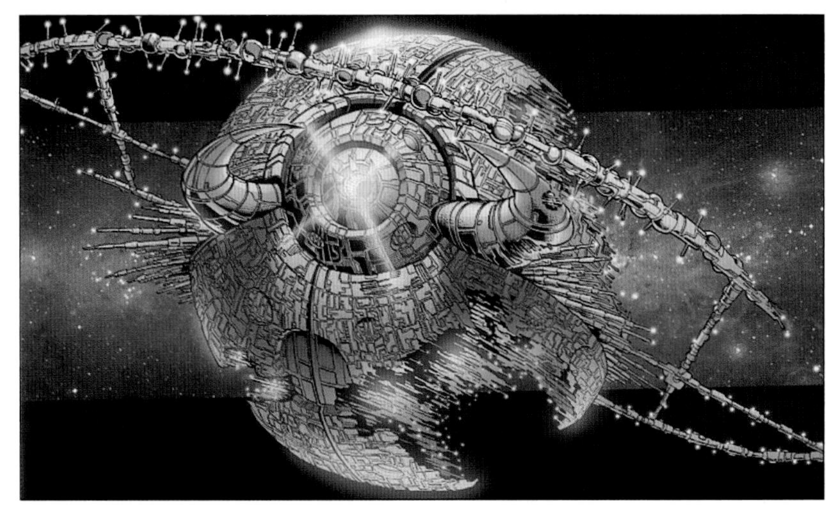

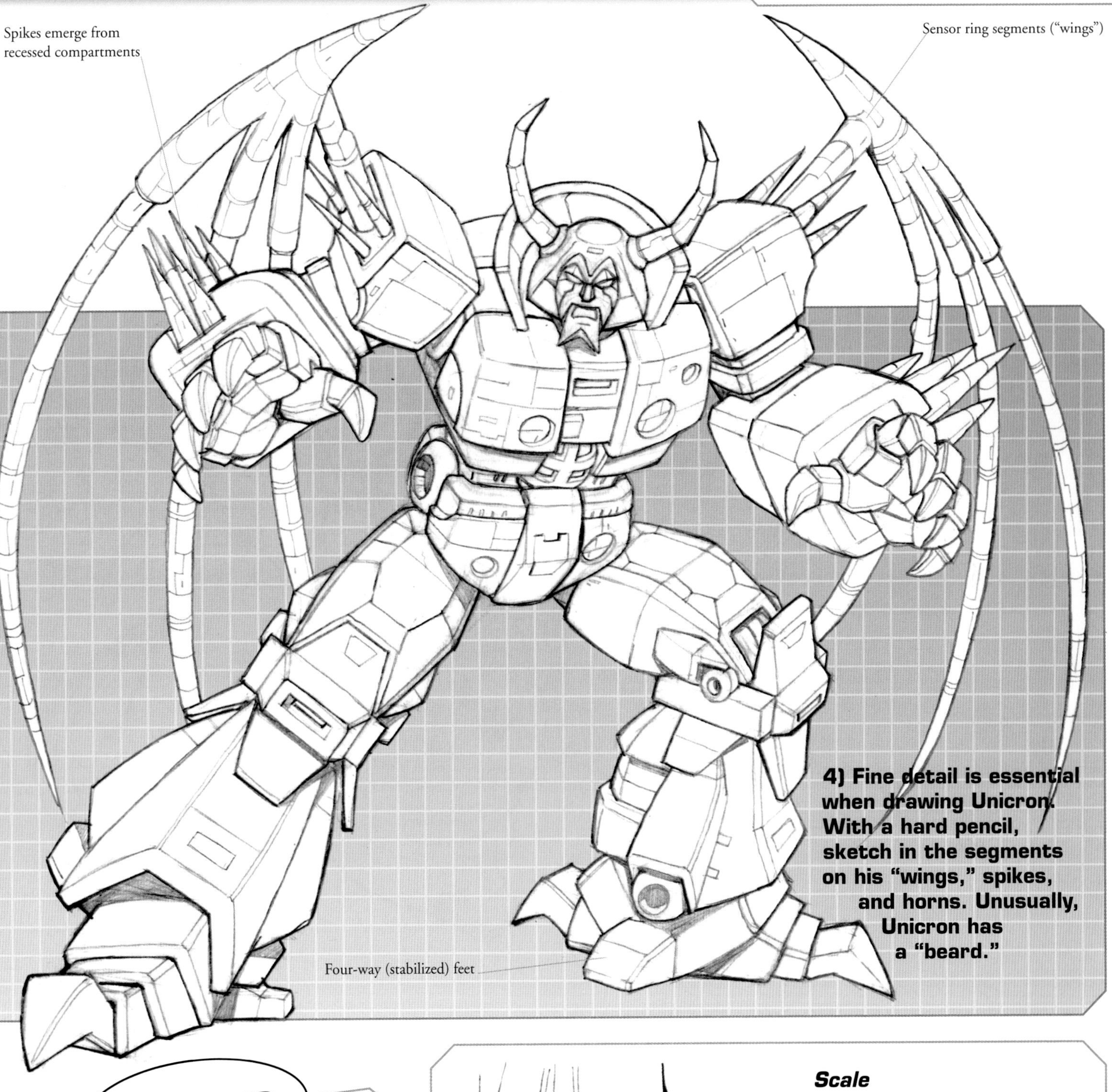

Spikes emerge from recessed compartments

Sensor ring segments ("wings")

4) Fine detail is essential when drawing Unicron. With a hard pencil, sketch in the segments on his "wings," spikes, and horns. Unusually, Unicron has a "beard."

Four-way (stabilized) feet

TIPS

When drawing Unicron add or suggest lots of small panel detail on his body. I always find it works well to depict him from extreme angles rather than just straight on. Extremely low or high angle shots with lots of foreshortening give the impression of size and add to his threatening presence.
Andrew Wildman

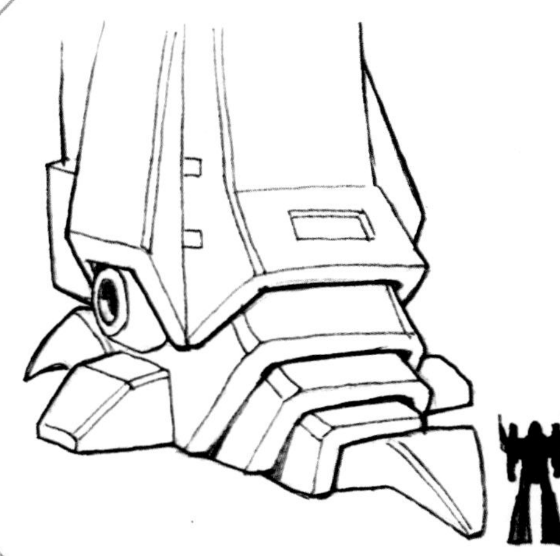

Scale

It's quite hard to conceive the true size of Unicron, who is, after all, of planetary scale. He's large enough that other TRANSFORMERS can exist (and move relatively freely) inside him. Even the largest of TRANSFORMERS (Devastator perhaps) would barely rise above the level of Unicron's front toe (see left).

BEAST WARS: MAXIMALS

THE CALL OF THE WILD

While beast modes for TRANSFORMERS were nothing new, the 1996 toy line (and CG-animated TV series) Beast Wars took that concept to a whole new level. When the descendents of the Autobots and the Decepticons crash-landed on prehistoric Earth they were all forced to adopt biomechanical beast modes in order to remain functional.

STEP-BY-STEP

Massive and largely immovable, Rhinox is one of Optimus Primal's most trusted lieutenants.

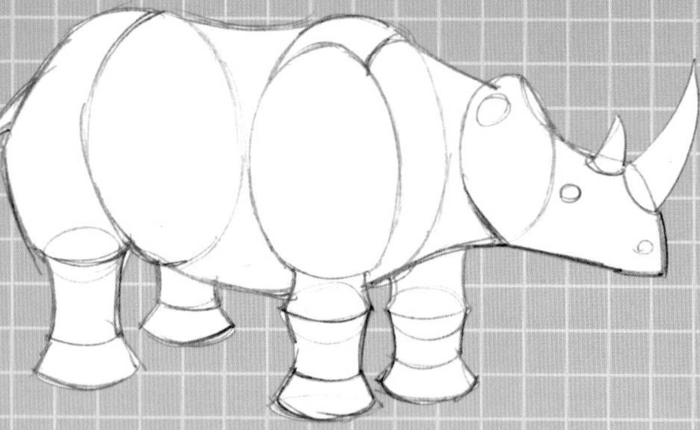

1) Drawing organic alt. modes requires different skills to rendering the sharp lines of a robot. The initial rough sketch is formed by using cylinders and ovals.

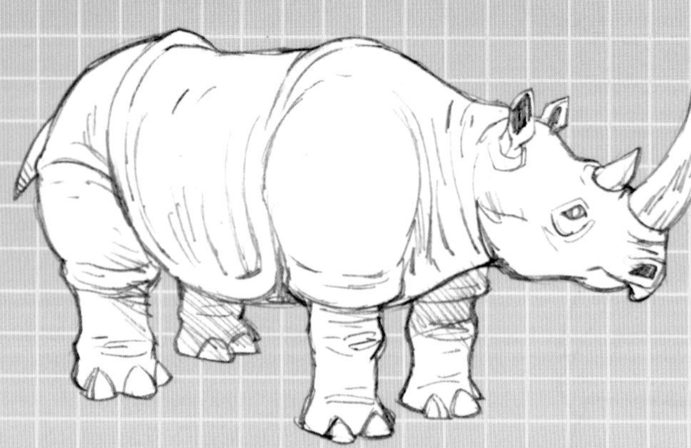

2) Over your outline, start to mould the actual shapes of a rhinoceros, adding the horns, ears, tail, and hooves. Shading gives texture to the hide or skin.

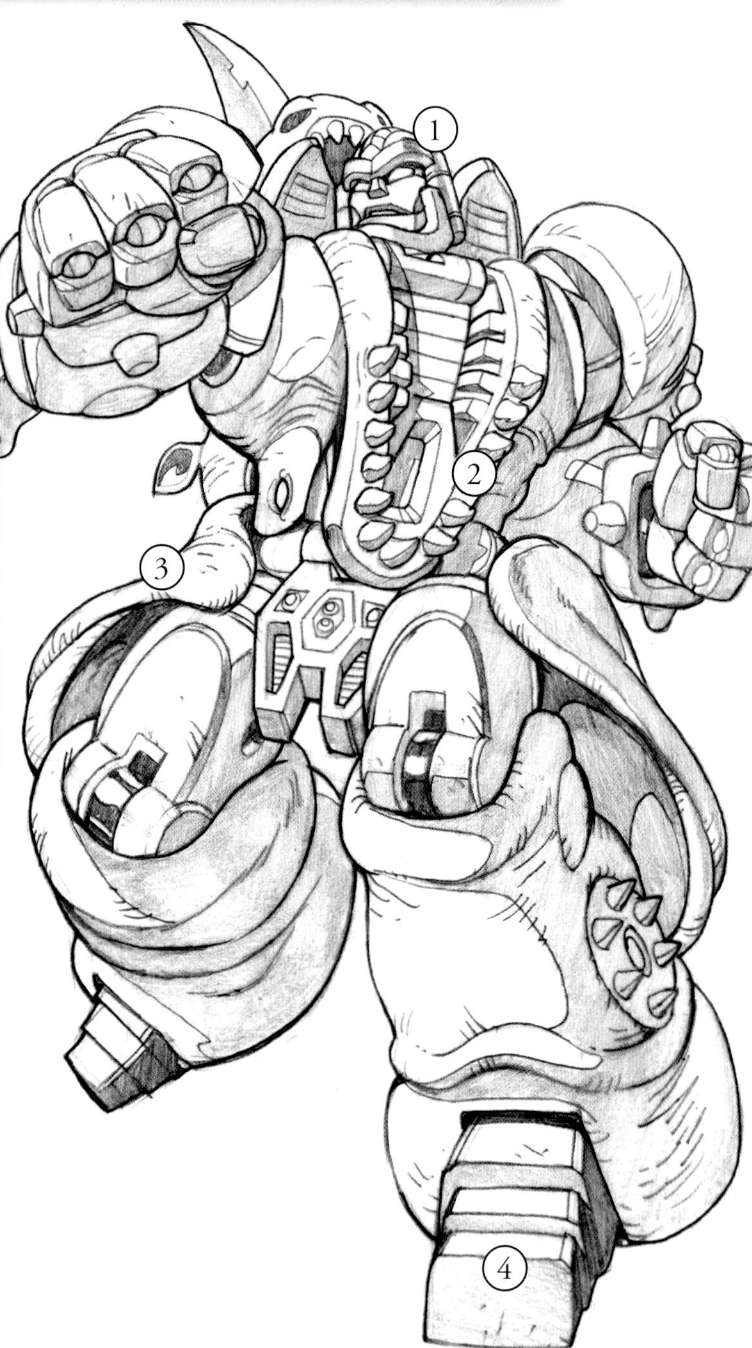

1. Rhinox's robot mode head tucks into a recessed cavity under his upper (beast mode) jaw.
2. Rhinox's lower (inner) jaw becomes his main chest armature, slotting in between his outer head segments.
3. Outer (beast mode) hide segments form rear protective robot mode leg guards.
4. Inset (robot mode) feet extend from recessed compartments.

STEP-BY-STEP

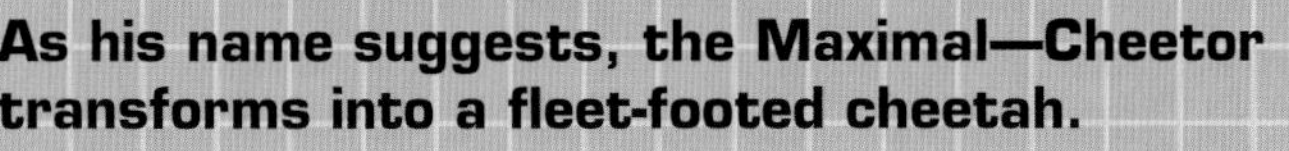

As his name suggests, the Maximal—Cheetor transforms into a fleet-footed cheetah.

1) Sketch in the main body segments, remembering to put in two joints in the back legs and add in a curve of tail.

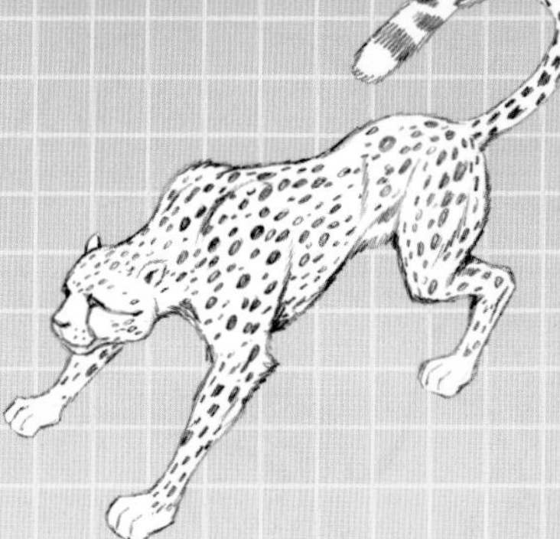

2) Now add in the detail and texture to create fur, erasing all the body segments and joints so the cheetah appears as one smooth, fluid entity.

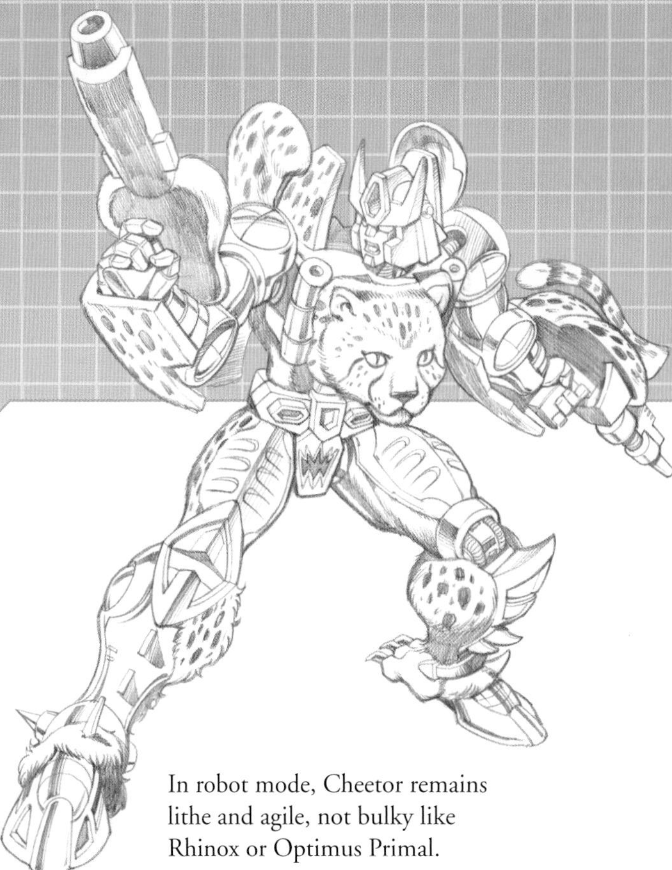

In robot mode, Cheetor remains lithe and agile, not bulky like Rhinox or Optimus Primal.

SKETCHBOOK

Fur, hide, and feathers take a lot of practice to get right. Try drawing a variety of animals and birds (from real life) in different poses, paying particular attention to the way their musculature and skin stretches and moves, and how fur or scales shift to those changes.

YOUR TURN

Take these four examples here and adapt them into their more stylized Maximal equivalents: the eagle (Silverbolt), the raptor (Dinobot), the gorilla (Optimus Primal), and the elephant (Ironhide).

BEAST WARS: PREDACONS

WHAT'S IN A NAME?

The name is the same, but the Megatron of Beast Wars is *not* the Generation 1 tyrant of old. However, this all-new Megatron is equally as dangerous and hell-bent on tearing apart the fragile alliance between the Maximals and the Predacons. His rogue band of Predacons includes Waspinator, Tarantulas, Scorponok, and Inferno.

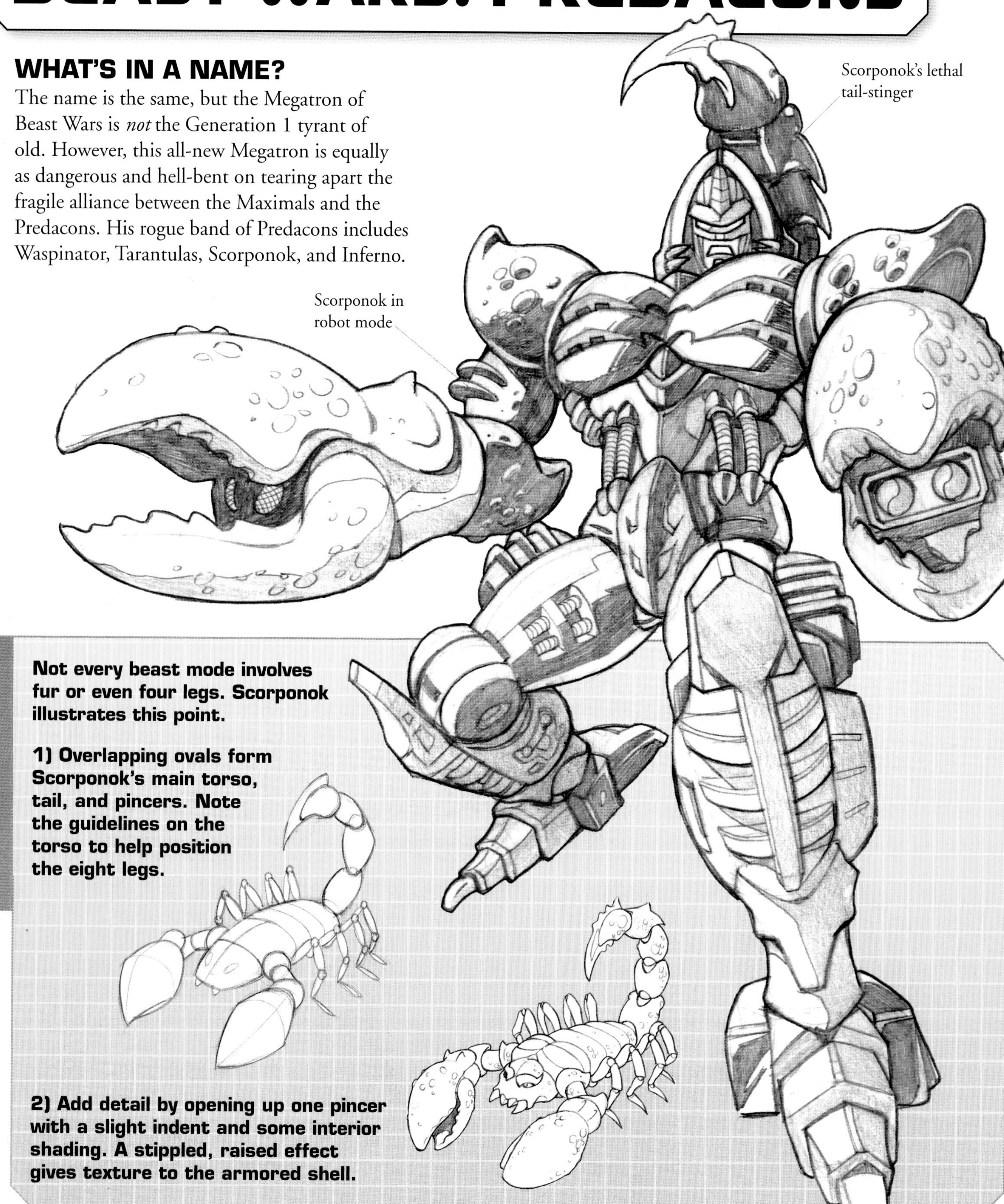

Scorponok's lethal tail-stinger

Scorponok in robot mode

STEP-BY-STEP

Not every beast mode involves fur or even four legs. Scorponok illustrates this point.

1) Overlapping ovals form Scorponok's main torso, tail, and pincers. Note the guidelines on the torso to help position the eight legs.

2) Add detail by opening up one pincer with a slight indent and some interior shading. A stippled, raised effect gives texture to the armored shell.

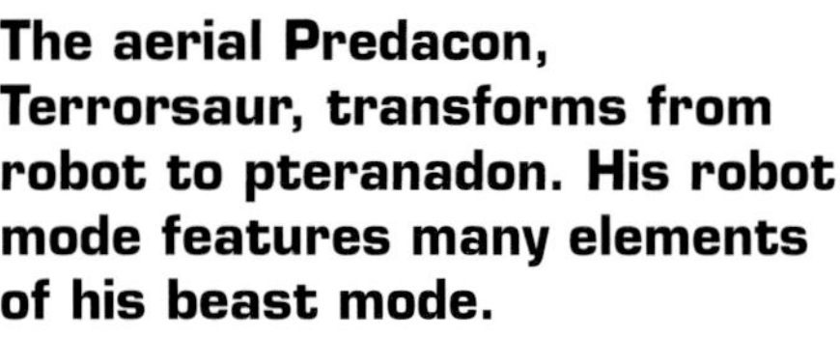

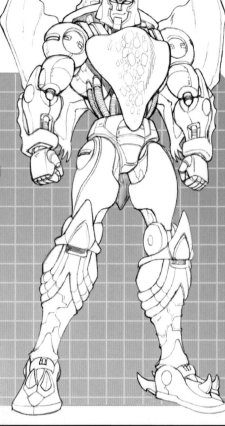

The aerial Predacon, Terrorsaur, transforms from robot to pteranadon. His robot mode features many elements of his beast mode.

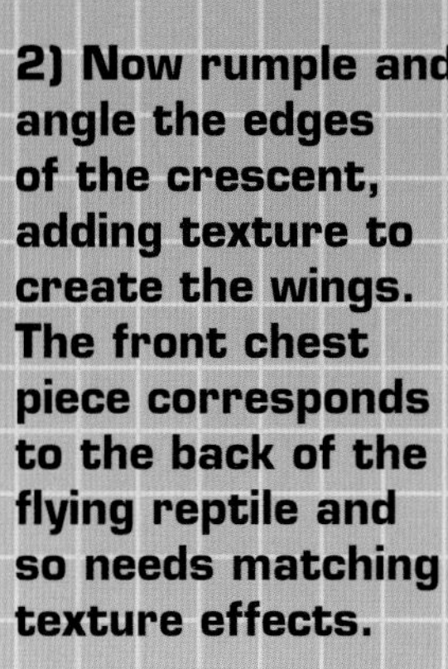

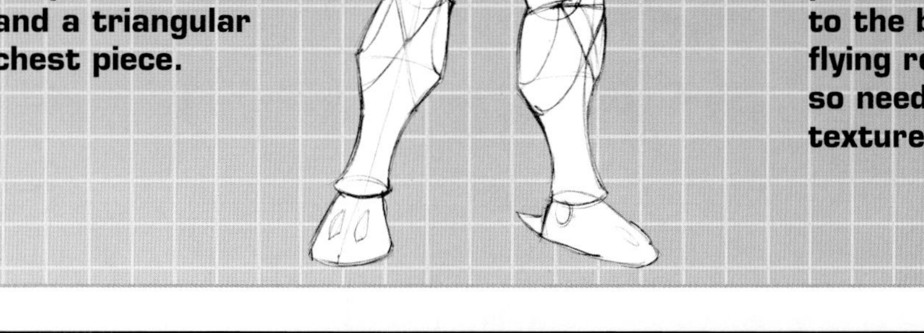

1) Sketch a stick figure and bulk it out like an armored human being. Then add a large crescent shape to the back and a triangular chest piece.

2) Now rumple and angle the edges of the crescent, adding texture to create the wings. The front chest piece corresponds to the back of the flying reptile and so needs matching texture effects.

SKETCHBOOK

Practice drawing as wide a variety of different animals, crustaceans, arachnids, and insects as possible. Once you see how the real creature is jointed, it'll be that much easier to apply it to your drawings. Here, we have Megatron, Tarantulas, Waspinator, and Rampage.

TIPS

To make evil Predacons more menacing and distinct from the heroic Maximals, feel free to use sharp and pointed parts for the armor's details, such as scales. Also fangs and claws can be emphasized to give a more aggressive look, even when they are in robot mode!

Guido Guidi

ARMADA & MINICONS

STARTING FROM SCRATCH

In 2002, TRANSFORMERS went back to basics, taking familiar characters and started over again, only this time with a twist. In the new toy line and series, the TRANSFORMERS came with power-boosting mini-TRANSFORMERS known as Minicons.

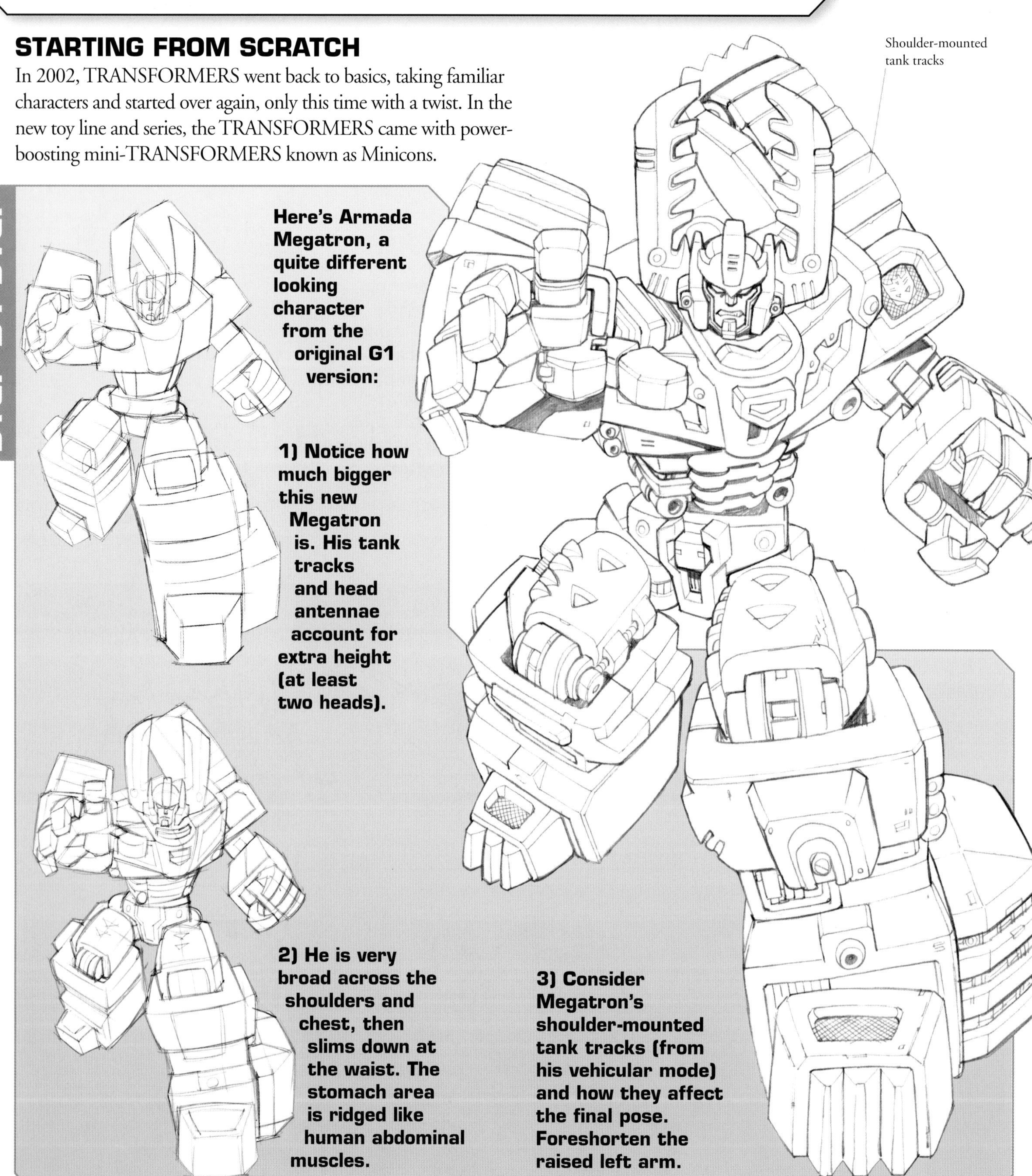

Here's Armada Megatron, a quite different looking character from the original G1 version:

1) Notice how much bigger this new Megatron is. His tank tracks and head antennae account for extra height (at least two heads).

2) He is very broad across the shoulders and chest, then slims down at the waist. The stomach area is ridged like human abdominal muscles.

3) Consider Megatron's shoulder-mounted tank tracks (from his vehicular mode) and how they affect the final pose. Foreshorten the raised left arm.

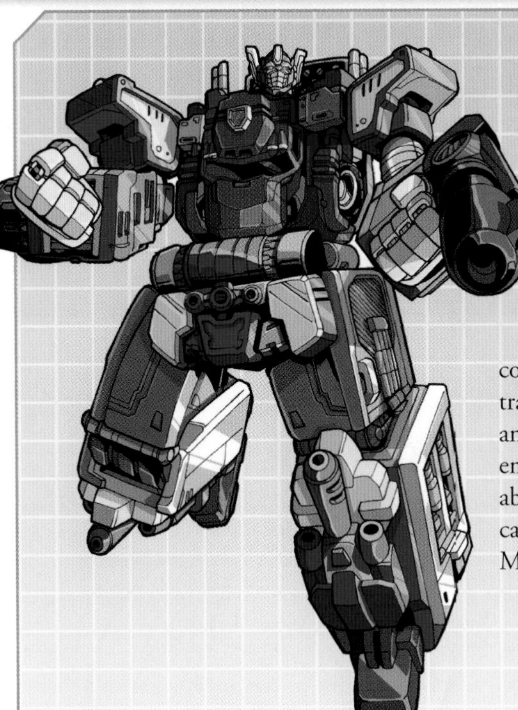

Optimus Prime

Or rather, "super" Optimus Prime. In this incarnation of the TRANSFORMERS saga, Prime can combine with his own trailer section to become an ultra-sized robot with enhanced firepower and abilities. In this form, he can connect with several Minicons at once.

Minicons

These diminutive 'bots are a different species altogether. The likes of Bonecrusher (pictured here) can transform into vehicular modes and attach themselves to a conventional TRANSFORMER, boosting their combined power level.

Sureshock

Many Minicons belong to small units or teams. Sureshock is part of the Street Action Team.

Iceberg

Along with Ransack and Dune Runner, Iceberg is a featured member of the Adventure Team. He transforms into a snowplough.

Runway

Runway belongs to the Air Defence Team and is one part of the Star Saber (see right).

Grindor

Another combiner, Grindor (along with Sureshock and High Wire) becomes one part of Perceptor, a larger robot.

The Star Saber

The combined form of the Air Defense Team (Runway, Sonar, and Jetstorm), the Star Saber is a weapon of supreme power.

TRANSFORMERS: ENERGON

ARMADA—EXPANDED

Transformers Energon continued the evolution of the TRANSFORMERS. Set 10 years after Armada's battle with Unicron, Energon introduced the Terrorcons and the Omnicons.

STEP-BY-STEP

Here's Energon Tidal Wave, a Decepticon with three alt. modes (gunboat, aircraft carrier, and aerial transport ship).

1) Tidal Wave is big, VERY big. Everything about him should emphasize the sheer scale of his towering robot mode. Pick an expansive pose with arms spread.

2) Now start to work in the detail. With three alt. modes, Tidal Wave has a number of different elements that need to be taken into account.

Familiar Faces

Here are three more characters from TRANSFORMERS Energon. All three are re-imagined versions of classic Generation 1 characters: Rodimus Prime, Ultra Magnus, and Grapple.

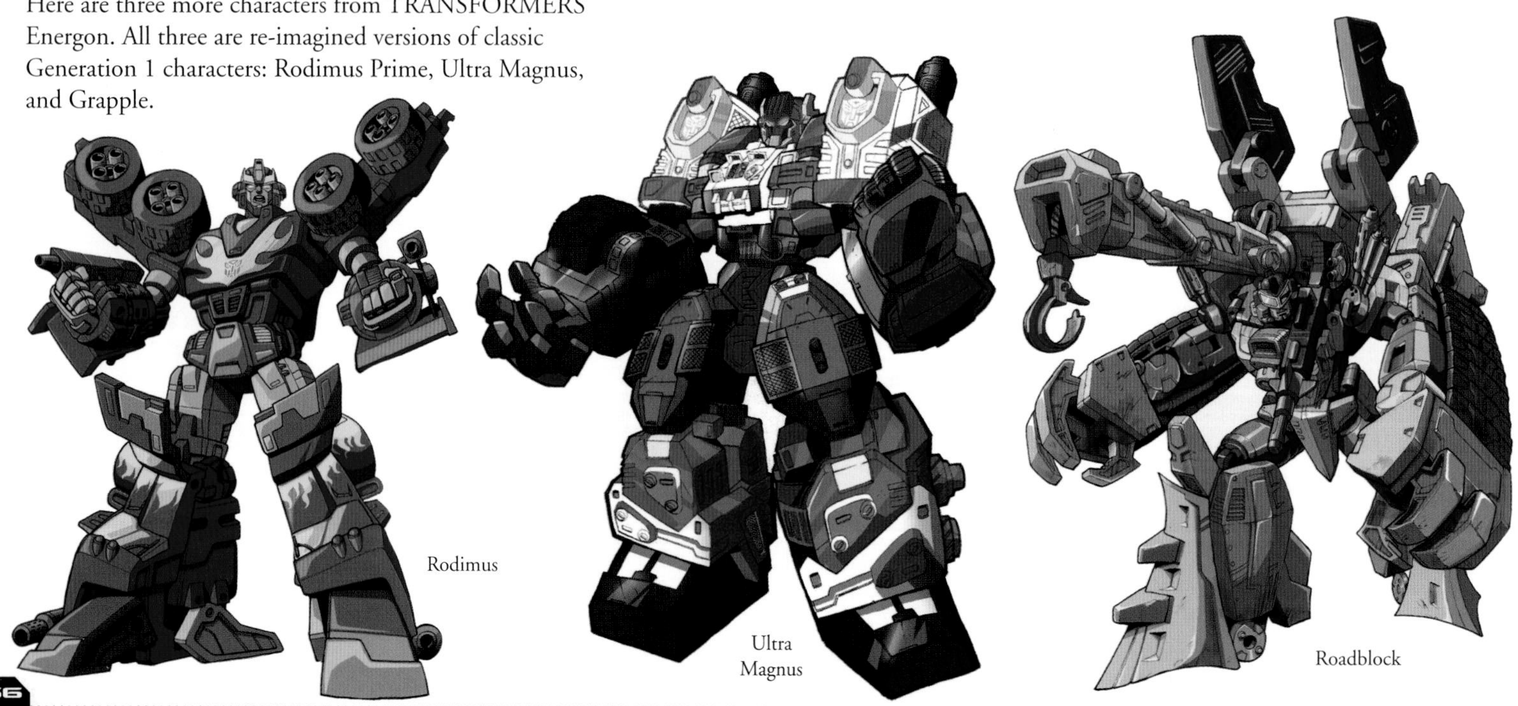

Rodimus

Ultra Magnus

Roadblock

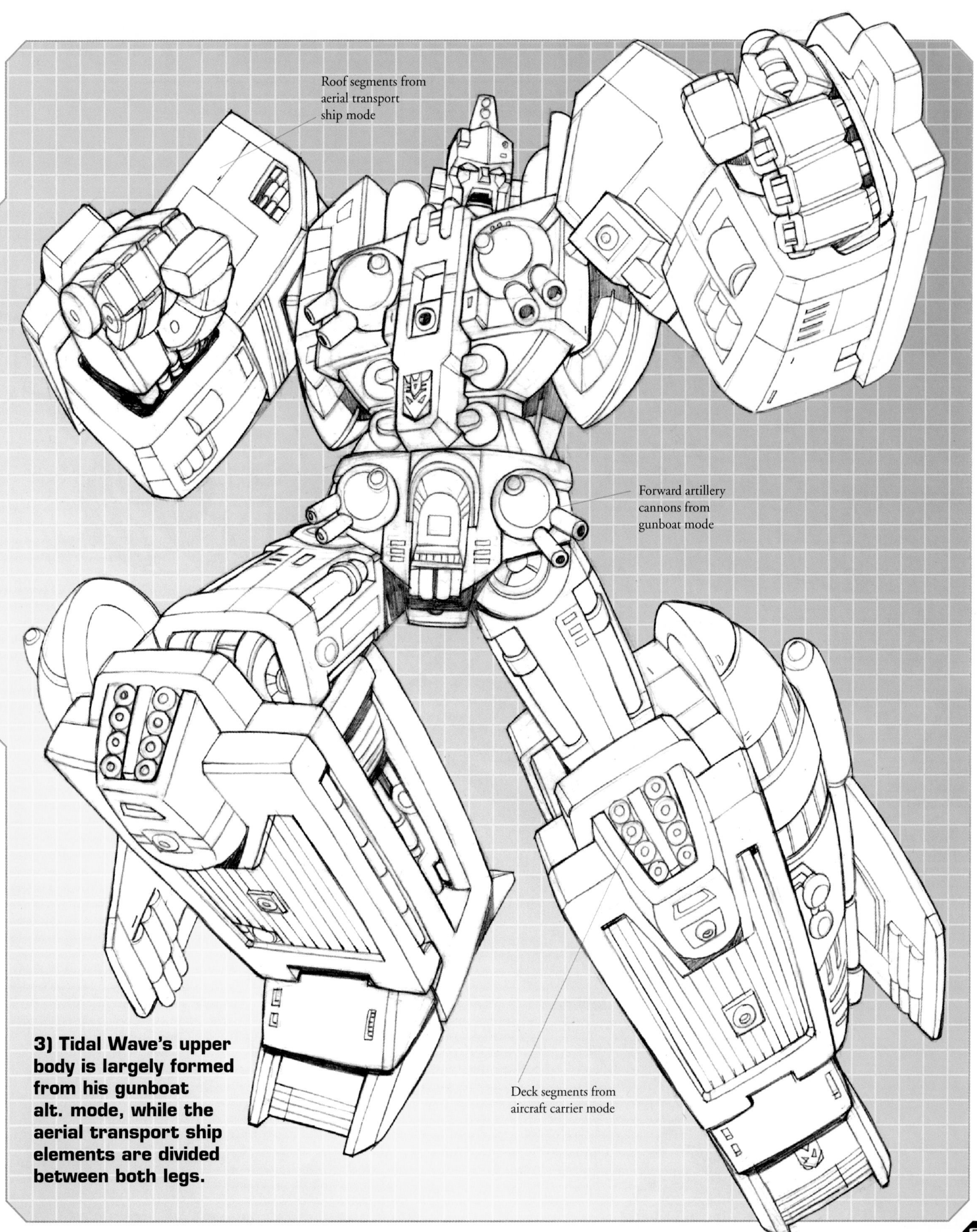

3) Tidal Wave's upper body is largely formed from his gunboat alt. mode, while the aerial transport ship elements are divided between both legs.

TRANSFORMERS: CYBERTRON

THE QUEST

When Cybertron is threatened by a vast, all-consuming black hole, the Autobots and Decepticons begin a search for the Cyber Planet Keys which can save Cybertron from destruction. The quest takes the TRANSFORMERS to strange new planets, including the Speed planet, the Giant planet, and the Jungle planet.

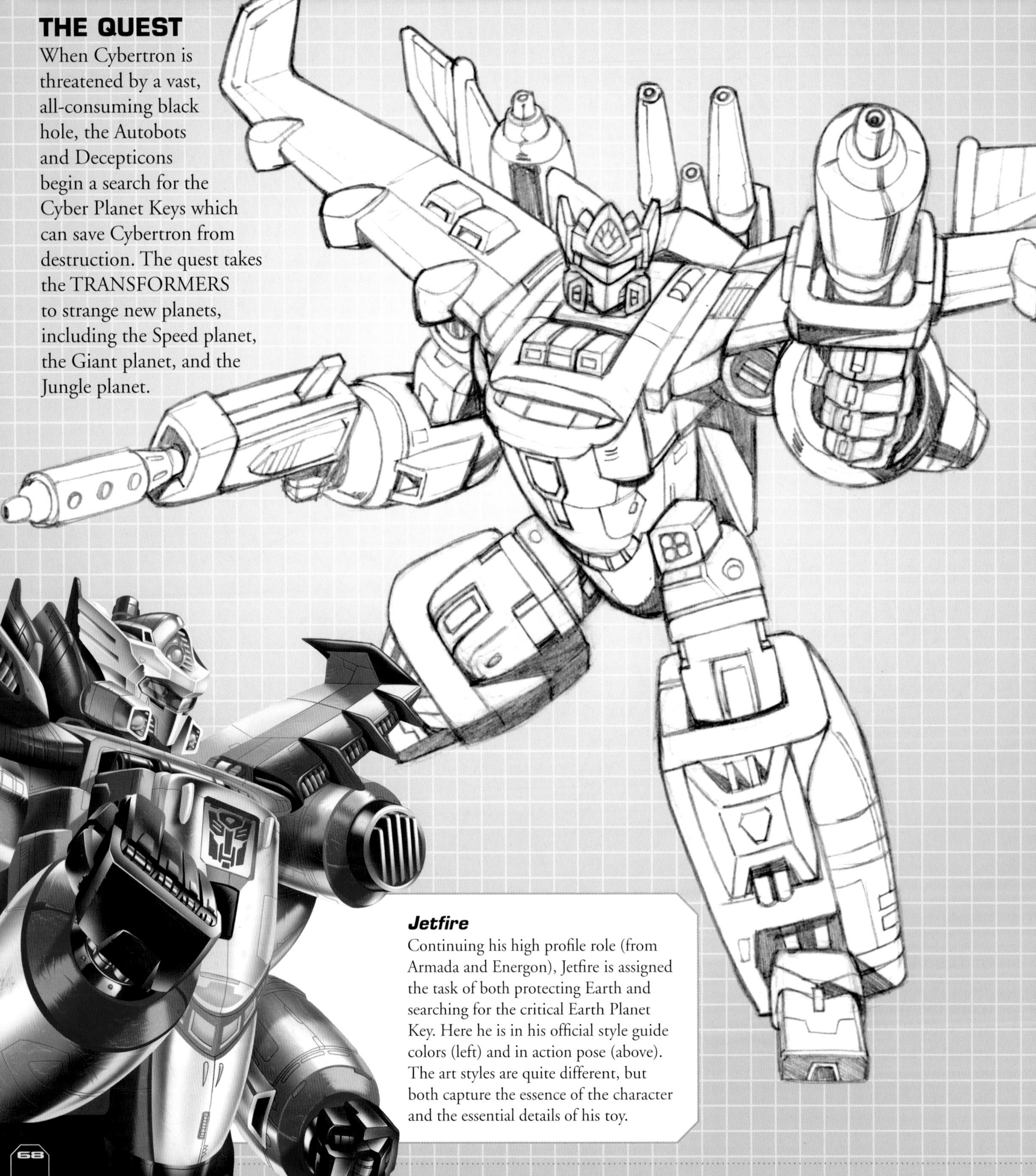

Jetfire

Continuing his high profile role (from Armada and Energon), Jetfire is assigned the task of both protecting Earth and searching for the critical Earth Planet Key. Here he is in his official style guide colors (left) and in action pose (above). The art styles are quite different, but both capture the essence of the character and the essential details of his toy.

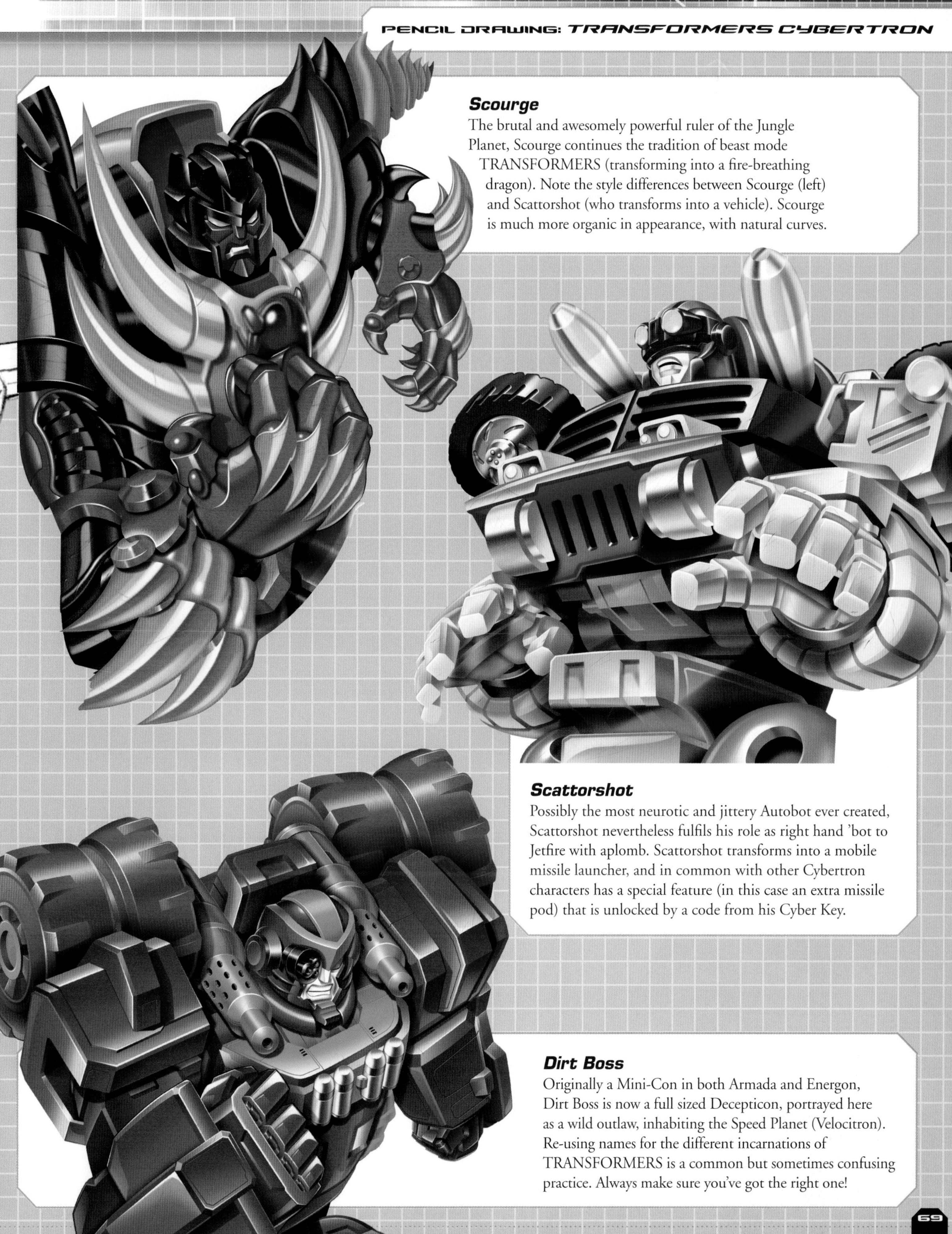

Scourge

The brutal and awesomely powerful ruler of the Jungle Planet, Scourge continues the tradition of beast mode TRANSFORMERS (transforming into a fire-breathing dragon). Note the style differences between Scourge (left) and Scattorshot (who transforms into a vehicle). Scourge is much more organic in appearance, with natural curves.

Scattorshot

Possibly the most neurotic and jittery Autobot ever created, Scattorshot nevertheless fulfils his role as right hand 'bot to Jetfire with aplomb. Scattorshot transforms into a mobile missile launcher, and in common with other Cybertron characters has a special feature (in this case an extra missile pod) that is unlocked by a code from his Cyber Key.

Dirt Boss

Originally a Mini-Con in both Armada and Energon, Dirt Boss is now a full sized Decepticon, portrayed here as a wild outlaw, inhabiting the Speed Planet (Velocitron). Re-using names for the different incarnations of TRANSFORMERS is a common but sometimes confusing practice. Always make sure you've got the right one!

STORMBRINGER

RETRO-DESIGNS

Before the TRANSFORMERS came to Earth, each of them possessed a robot and alt. mode more suited to the alien environment of their home planet, Cybertron. Artist Don Figueroa was given the job of retro-designing the characters, working backwards from their "classic" incarnations.

Optimus Prime

In Stormbringer, Don Figueroa opted for a more militaristic Optimus Prime, with a veritable arsenal of built-on or hand-held weaponry, including shoulder-mounted cannons on roller tracks and arm-mounted twin blasters. In the final, climactic battle with Thunderwing, Prime brings all weapons to bear, with truly devastating results.

Centurion Drones

On the war-torn surface of Cybertron, non-sentient drone troopers provide armed security for Bludgeon's secret base of operations. Don Figueroa designed these implacable engines of destruction, with multiple alt. modes.

Bludgeon

Though little re-design work was necessary for Bludgeon's outer shell (seen here), Don Figueroa created a new version of the inner robot for Stormbringer, one that combined elements of the original inner robot and the distinctive outer shell. Both incarnations of Bludgeon feature an energo-sword.

THUNDERWING

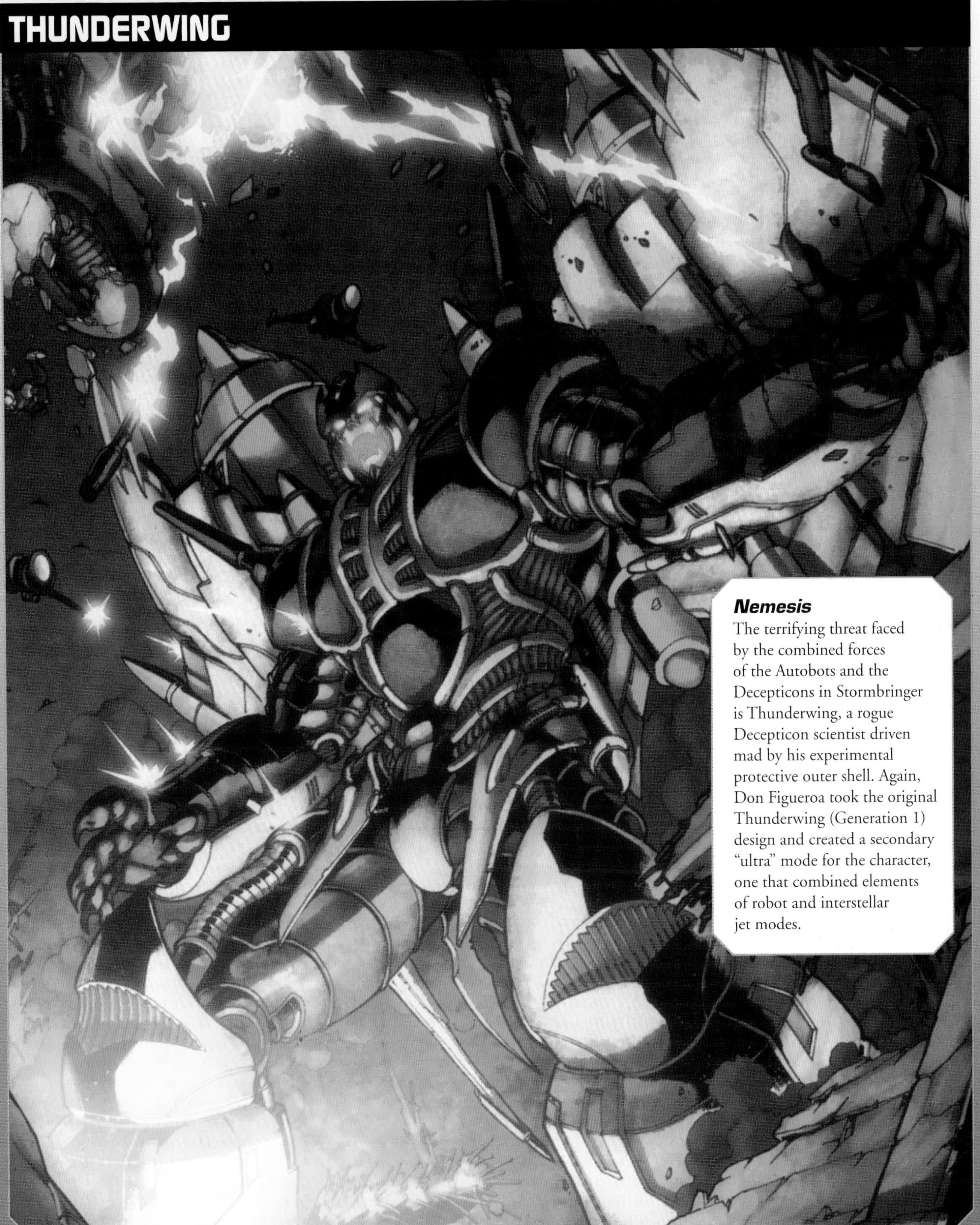

Nemesis

The terrifying threat faced by the combined forces of the Autobots and the Decepticons in Stormbringer is Thunderwing, a rogue Decepticon scientist driven mad by his experimental protective outer shell. Again, Don Figueroa took the original Thunderwing (Generation 1) design and created a secondary "ultra" mode for the character, one that combined elements of robot and interstellar jet modes.

MEGATRON

Few villains can outdo Megatron when it comes to the sheer unchecked pursuit of power. From the very earliest TRANSFORMERS stories, it was clear that Megatron was a force to be reckoned with, as an all-conquering tyrant with little capacity or inclination for mercy. The Decepticon Commander-in-Chief respected (but not feared) only one other being in the whole vast universe, and that was Optimus Prime, his greatest nemesis. Let's get up close and personal with Megatron.

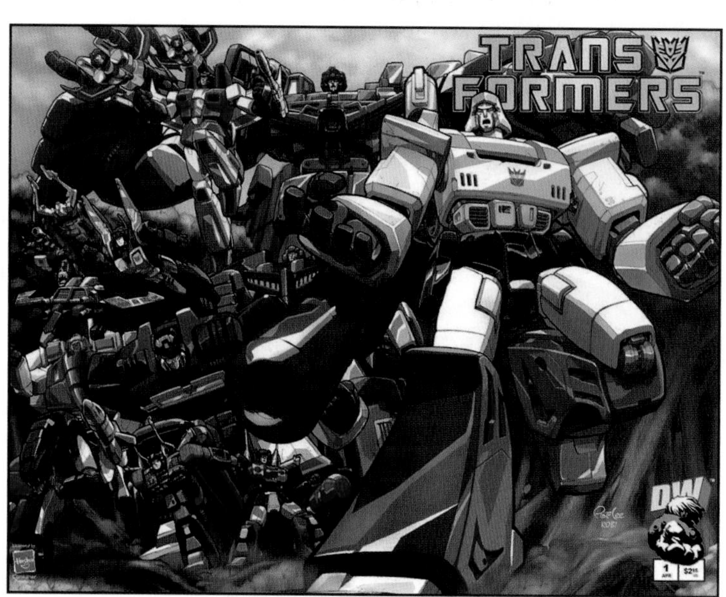

WAR AND PEACE #1
Decepticons galore on one of the five covers for issue #1 of Dreamwave's second G1 story arc. The Decepticon cover was mirrored by an Autobot variant. Art by Pat Lee.

CHARACTER HISTORY

In the days before the great civil war between the Autobots and the Decepticons, Megatron slowly and patiently cemented his personal power base, selecting the deadliest and most fearsome warriors from the many who came to fight in his secret underground arenas on Cybertron. Those who, like him, wished for an end to peace and the dawn of tyranny and oppression, became known as Decepticons, and when they were suitably armed and ready, they struck! With Megatron at the forefront of every campaign, more and more rallied to his call. Before the Autobots knew what was happening, Cybertron had all but fallen to Megatron. Nothing now could stop him… or so it seemed!

CYBERTRON FORM
On Cybertron, Megatron transformed not into a handgun (as per his Earth incarnation) but a lethal and heavily armored Hyper-Tank, one possessed of truly devastating firepower. This Cybertronian form was first seen in issue #1 of *The War Within* (2002).

TIPS

Megatron's forearm cannon is the most recognizable element on the character. It is important to keep his cannon in proportion, and not make it too large. As mechanical as the TRANSFORMERS maybe, their eyes also convey a lot of their personality. Pay attention to how different shapes of eyes can reflect different personalities.

E.J. Su

ROUGH PENCIL DRAWING

Before starting in on the figure drawing itself, be sure to rough out your Megatron pose in very loose stick figure form, paying particular attention to his arm-mounted fusion cannon. Because of its length, bend the right elbow joint so the cannon is almost vertical.

ROUGH PENCIL DRAWING

Before starting in on the figure drawing itself, be sure to rough out your Megatron pose in very loose stick figure form, paying particular attention to his arm-mounted fusion cannon. Because of its length, bend the right elbow joint so the cannon is almost vertical.

FINAL PENCIL DRAWING

Once the main figure is complete, and you've carefully worked out the perspective on the fusion cannon and the foreshortening of the left arm, then start adding in the detail and shading. Add a menacing dark shadow above and around Megatron's eyes.

DETAILS

FUSION CANNON

Megatron's primary weapon is his arm-mounted fusion cannon, which can tap other-dimensional energy from the heart of a black hole, channeling it into a blast capable of shattering whole mountains. Its internal reaction chamber processes combustible matter from the collapsed star, mixing it with plasma and unleashing it with focused precision as a particle beam. Few foes survive a direct hit.

HOLO-WEAPONRY

Something of a living weapon himself, Megatron does however have other armaments at his disposal. As well as his fusion cannon and a back-up (rear-mounted) mortar launcher, Megatron can call upon sophisticated (melee) holo-weaponry. His right hand is detachable, and holo-emitters in his wrist generate a deadly array of solid light extensions.

ALTERNATIVE MODE

Not only can Megatron transform into a likeness of a Walther P-38 handgun, as he does so he can displace (into inter-dimensional space) much of his overall body mass, thereby shrinking in size. In this fashion he can be wielded either by other Decepticons or (at minimum size) by a human being. However, even at reduced size, a single blast can still atomize even the largest target.

Megatron: full transformation. From robot mode to gun mode in four stages.

FINAL INKED DRAWING

Apply heavy black areas in and around the visible joints and lightly fleck areas of the body with ink to add a rough quality to the metal surfaces. Finally, consider your light source and apply any areas of shadow cast by the extended fusion cannon.

Keep facial detail spare, using the minimum of hard black lines and shadow to maximum effect.

An uneven edge to this area of shade gives the effect of curvature to the fusion cannon.

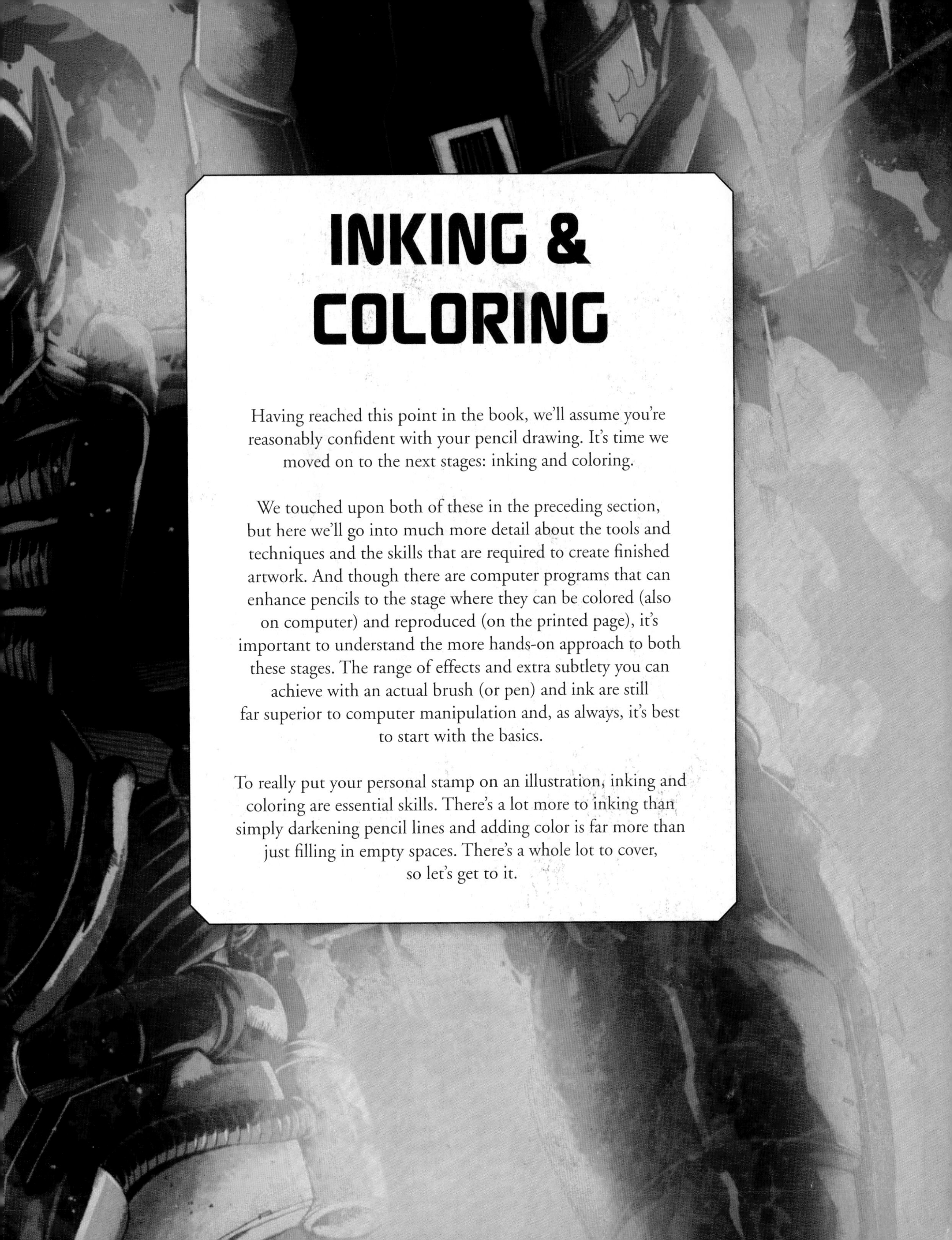

INKING & COLORING

Having reached this point in the book, we'll assume you're reasonably confident with your pencil drawing. It's time we moved on to the next stages: inking and coloring.

We touched upon both of these in the preceding section, but here we'll go into much more detail about the tools and techniques and the skills that are required to create finished artwork. And though there are computer programs that can enhance pencils to the stage where they can be colored (also on computer) and reproduced (on the printed page), it's important to understand the more hands-on approach to both these stages. The range of effects and extra subtlety you can achieve with an actual brush (or pen) and ink are still far superior to computer manipulation and, as always, it's best to start with the basics.

To really put your personal stamp on an illustration, inking and coloring are essential skills. There's a lot more to inking than simply darkening pencil lines and adding color is far more than just filling in empty spaces. There's a whole lot to cover, so let's get to it.

EQUIPMENT

INKING

Used to add depth, contrast, and sharpness to a comic page or single illustration, inking is an essential tool for the up and coming artist. Pens, brushes, and markers can enhance lines and draw out the essential detail.

Dip pens

The (removable) nib is dipped in ink to use. The nib's point is flexible, allowing for different line widths and effects as you ink.

Technical pens

The ink is contained in an interior cartridge and the tips vary in thickness, depending on the width of line required.

Dip pen and nibs

Technical pen

Felt-tip pens or markers

Marker pens and felt tips are especially useful for larger areas of black, but can brown or fade with age. As with technical pens, they are available in wide range of tip thicknesses.

Felt-tip

Fine felt-tip

Wide felt-tip

Biro

Brushes

Many artists prefer to work with a brush. These come in a wide range from fine to thick, and the bristles can be either synthetic or natural hair. Always remember to clean brushes thoroughly in water immediately after use to avoid clogging.

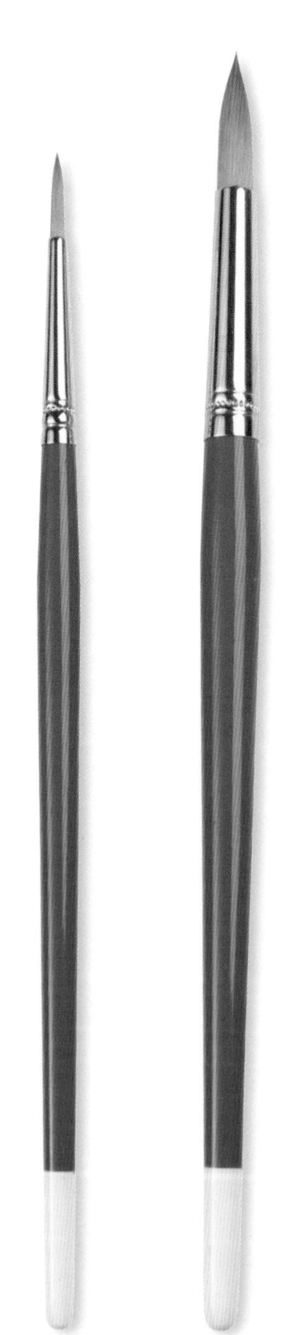

Ink

There are many makes and varieties of ink, and these do differ in terms of their thickness or density. Ideally, thick black ink that covers well and doesn't clog or appear washed out on the page should be used.

Correction fluid

Almost as indispensable as the eraser, correction fluid or tape can applied to inked artwork either to cover up mistakes or create effects such as a star-filled night sky.

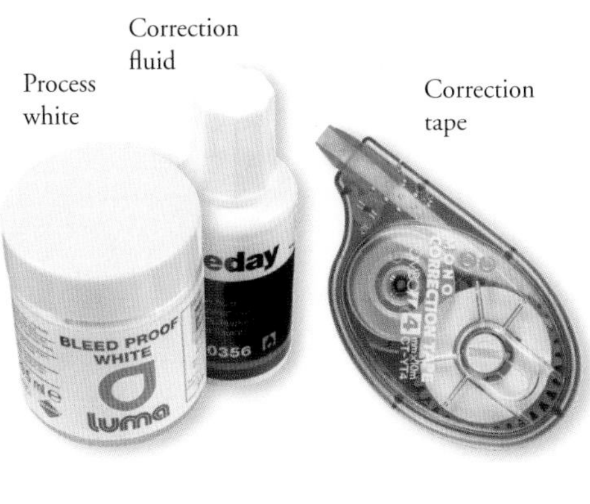

TIPS

After I have sketched (I use a 2B or 4B pencil) and cleaned up the penciling with a mechanical pencil, I ink in the lines with a pen. I prefer to use technical pens as I can work faster with them than with dip pens and brushes. I usually use 0.1, 0.5, and 0.8 thicknesses of pen to get a really consistent, professional-looking finish.

Marcelo Matere

Coloring

A wide variety of coloring tools are available to the artist. Before the computer era, markers, crayons, and colour pencils were used to create a colour rough of the page, before paint was applied with a brush or airbrush (often onto special, color-receptive paper like Kentmere).

Paint

Paint comes in four distinct varieties: oils, acrylics, watercolors, and gouache. Oils are easy to mix and manipulate, while acrylics are less flexible but dry faster. Watercolors soak deep into the paper and thereafter are difficult to alter, and gouache can be thinned to create a watercolor effect or applied at full thickness.

INKING EFFECTS

HARD LINES

All the drama and intensity of your pencil art can be further enhanced with the careful application of strong inked lines. Whether it's creating the polished sheen of battle armor or the rough texture of fractured, crumbling stone or simply lifting your figure out of a busy background, you will find that inking makes the whole image come to life on the page. Here are just a few of the effects that can be achieved.

The Gathering Storm
The moody menace of Thunderwing (from the cover of TRANSFORMERS Stormbringer #1) is accentuated here by large areas of solid black inks, creating an almost negative image. The areas of background flame are inked only very lightly, in anticipation of the color (flame) effects to come. Art by Don Figueroa, colours by Josh Burcham.

TEXTURES

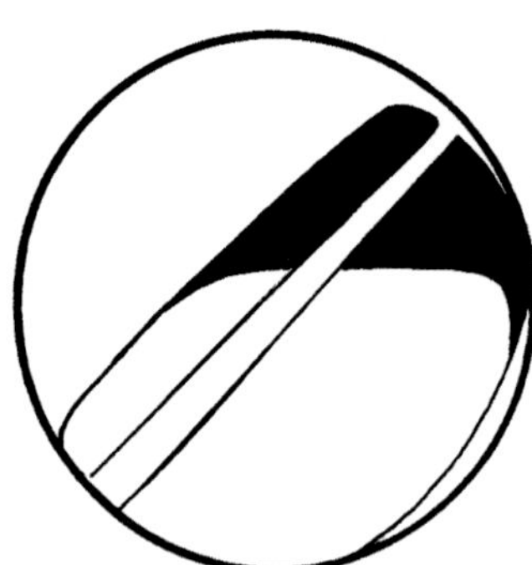

Glass
This area of solid black, shot through with lighter black lines and curved inwards, gives the impression of a polished or reflective surface.

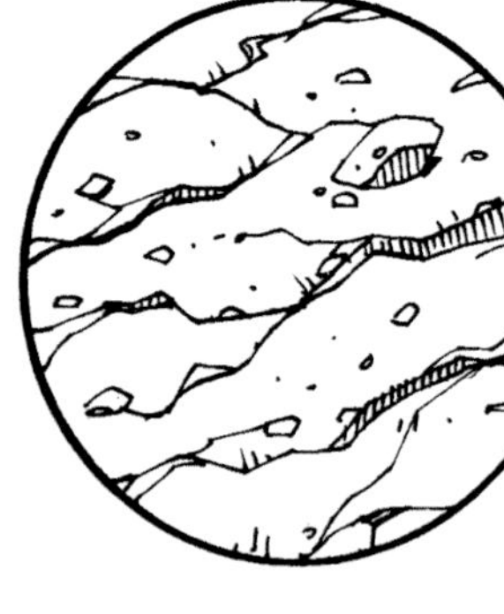

Stone
Fine, light pen work and shading with just a few vertical flecks creates the impression of cracks.

Wood
Thin and thick lines combine with slight feathering to create a gnarled surface.

Chome
Lines of decreasing thickness, applied with a brush or pens, create a shiny metallic effect.

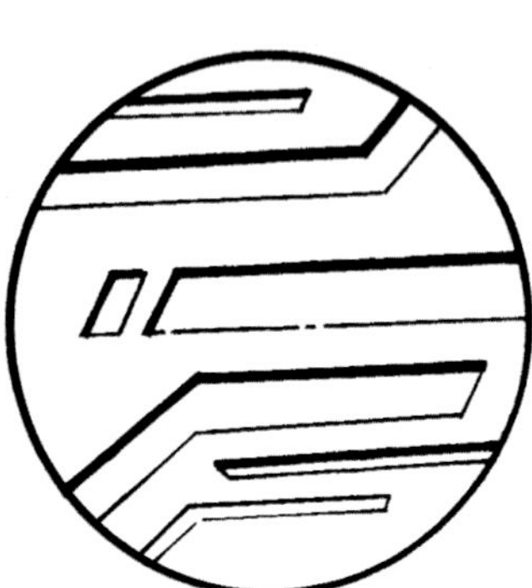

Embossing
Strong lines across two edges of a given shape create a sense of differing depths to the selected area. Useful for raised insignias.

TIPS

When inking your TRANSFORMERS drawings, it's usually best to use pens rather than brushes to ink the robots themselves. Pens give you more sharp and consistent lines, which look great on hard-edged robots, buildings, and technology. Brushes give you a more fluid line, and are excellent for inking people and natural landscapes.

Nick Roche

Light Inking
Here, the artist is relying on the color stage to flesh out this Megatron image. There's little definition to the figure and little or no texture to the metal.

Medium Inking
This is a standard inked version of the same image. There's weight and texture to the figure, and the raised hand and fusion cannon pop out of the frame at you.

Heavy Inking
Here, the artist has fully rendered the figure, adding in all the shading, cross-hatching, and feathering (and even a glint effect on the barrel of the fusion cannon).

SILHOUETTES

He's Behind You!
One way of separating foreground and background characters and at the same time heightening the drama of an image is to use a full or partial silhouette. Here, Devastator looms over Optimus Prime, appearing as a solid black figure with just a few subtle (white) highlights. The version on the left has the two figures bleeding into one another, the blacks meshing, whereas on the right, the artist has left a thin white border between them to really lift Prime out. The same effect is created by running a thin line of process white around the Prime figure.

COLOR

COLOR PROPERTIES

Light, when reflected off a given object, is perceived by the human eye as color. That color has three distinct properties: hue, intensity, and value. Hue is basically the name of the color, while intensity measures a color's strength and purity, and value describes a scale of lightness and darkness.

COLOR WHEEL

There are three primary colors: yellow, blue, and red, which form the basis of all other colors. This so-called color theory is best displayed on a color wheel (right). On the wheel, the primary colors form three points of a triangle. Midway between them are the secondary colors, which are mixed from the primary colors. In between are the tertiary colors, which are made by mixing primary and secondary hues.

Primary
Tertiary
Secondary
Tertiary
Primary
Tertiary
Secondary
Tertiary
Primary (showing shades of the color)
Tertiary
Secondary
Tertiary

Color Psychology

How colors interact, on one illustration or a whole page of panel-to-panel artwork, and affect the viewer, is a psychology all of its own. Here's a quick guide to some of the dos and don'ts.

Monochrome Colors

If you select a color from the color wheel and use different shades of that color, it will create a subtler contrast than using two opposing colors.

Analogue Colors

Now if you choose two colors next to each other in the color wheel, they contrast more than monochrome colors but are more harmonious than complementary colors.

Complementary Colors

Complementary colors (like purple and yellow) are directly opposite each other in the color wheel, and when used together, make each other appear more vibrant on the page.

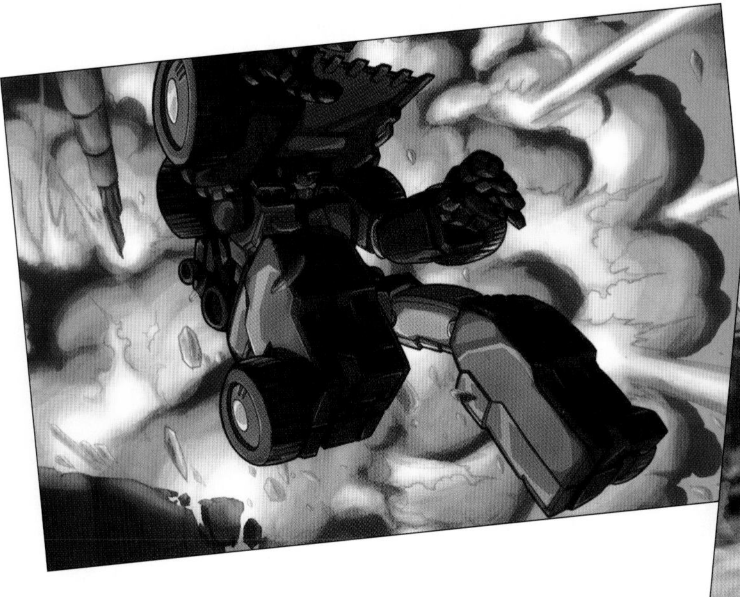

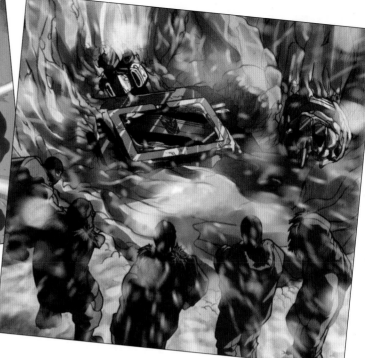

Hot and Cold Colors

As you can see from the above two images, some colors (reds, yellows, and oranges) evoke a feeling of warmth, while blues, purples, and whites create the opposite effect; that of icy cold. Neutral colors can be used to create a more subtle mood.

1) At the pencils stage, the artist is aware of how much of the detail and shading can be left to the inks stage.

2) The artist keeps his line work to a minimum where he anticipates color will be used.

3) As you can see from the finished (colored) cover, the artist has been careful not to do unnecessary work in the earlier stages that the color stage would just duplicate.

FROM START TO FINISH

There been a lot to take onboard in this and the previous section, but by now you should be feeling confident enough to progress your illustration through from pencils to inks to finished color. Whether you are doing all the stages yourself or handing off latter stages to an inker or colorist, it's important to plan ahead (see above) right from the word go.

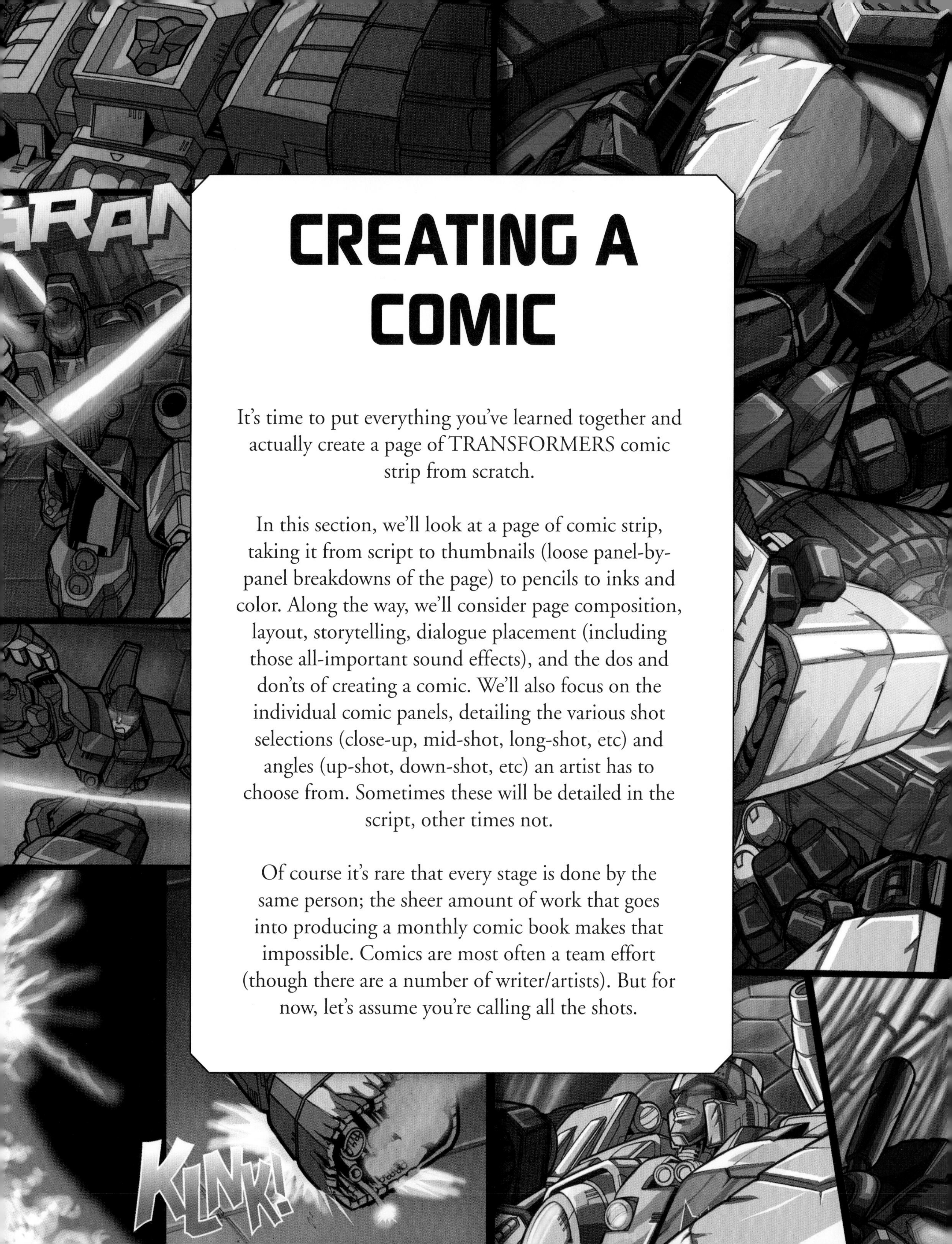

CREATING A COMIC

It's time to put everything you've learned together and actually create a page of TRANSFORMERS comic strip from scratch.

In this section, we'll look at a page of comic strip, taking it from script to thumbnails (loose panel-by-panel breakdowns of the page) to pencils to inks and color. Along the way, we'll consider page composition, layout, storytelling, dialogue placement (including those all-important sound effects), and the dos and don'ts of creating a comic. We'll also focus on the individual comic panels, detailing the various shot selections (close-up, mid-shot, long-shot, etc) and angles (up-shot, down-shot, etc) an artist has to choose from. Sometimes these will be detailed in the script, other times not.

Of course it's rare that every stage is done by the same person; the sheer amount of work that goes into producing a monthly comic book makes that impossible. Comics are most often a team effort (though there are a number of writer/artists). But for now, let's assume you're calling all the shots.

SHOTS & ANGLES

STORYTELLING

Good storytelling and page composition are essential skills for the comic book artist. In a relatively small space, a lot has to be established or conveyed, which requires the artist to select the most suitable or dramatic angle to best illustrate the scene or action called for in the script. Here's a guide to some of the unique terminology that you might come across in a script.

Long Shot

Also known as an establishing shot, this is a wide (sometimes panoramic) view of the entire scene, one that includes plenty of background detail, any immediate surroundings, and the position of the main character or characters within them. Often, a new scene will start with a long shot and then move in closer for subsequent panels. However, used in reverse, the artist can set up a dramatic reveal.

Medium Shot

The medium or mid-shot moves the reader closer in on the focal character, allowing plenty of room for dialogue while still highlighting the character himself. Some background is still visible here, but the emphasis has shifted more to the character. More often than not, a medium shot will crop the lower legs or even waist, according to preference or script detail.

Close-up

Used to convey emotion or simply to draw attention to some detail of the character's appearance, a close-up shot features hardly any background at all (and sometimes none at all). Here, we're up close and personal, the camera intimate with the subject. This progression, from long shot to close-up, is the most fundamental storytelling tool, allowing the reader to understand the environment before focusing in on the character.

Up Shot

In the image (far left), the camera (or perspective) is from a low angle, giving the character immediate stature. With almost no facial detail, he appears powerful and imposing—a force to be reckoned with. This is known as an up shot.

Down Shot

In this image (left), the camera is above the focal character looking down. This intensifies the feeling of something important below, or if he were looking upwards—above. Alternatively, this technique can be used to suggest the point of view of a taller character.

Framing

Where to place your character or characters within the panel border is more common sense than acquired skill. Of the two examples, one has Blaster badly cropped and off centre, while the other has Blaster more central to the panel with clear space between the top of his head and the upper panel border and available (dead) space for dialogue, top right.

Inset Panels

Including a second (inset) panel within a larger panel can help to show two different angles or aspects of the same scene, or perhaps a close up of a crucial detail from the larger panel. Here, two sides of a conversation (via a comm. link) are shown, so we can immediately see who Optimus Prime is talking to.

SCRIPT & THUMBNAILS

VISUALIZATION

Comics are a visual medium. It's not enough to be just a writer. The greatest writer in the world might be the world's worst comic book writer, simply because they didn't properly visualize how their words would translate to each page of artwork.

Transformers #XXX
Script for 22 pages
Joe Writer (444) 555-0000

Panel One
Up angle on Grimlock (dinosaur mode). He has his jaws gripped tight on Devastator's right hand, teeth sunk in deep. Devastator (in pain) is trying to shake him off, to no avail.

1. DEVASTATOR: **EAAGH!** LET… **GO!**

Panel Two
Down angle on: Slag (dino mode), Sludge (robot), and Snarl (dino mode). They're looking up, mouths open.

2. SLAG: WHAT'S HE **DOING? DEVASTATOR** WILL CRUSH HIM LIKE A MECHA-BUG!
SLUDGE: HEY—HE'S **GRIMLOCK**.
SNARL: WHICH SAYS IT **ALL** REALLY.

Panel Three
Above (aerial angle), Swoop (dino mode) powers in, underwing missiles firing, impacting on Devastator's left flank.

SWOOP: ARE YOU LOT JUST GOING TO STAND THERE?
SFX: **THWOOM!**
SWOOP (2): OR ARE YOU GOING TO **DO** SOMETHING!

Panel Four
Ground level angle, as the Dinobots charge towards us, Sludge with his en-ergo-sword pulled back to strike, Slag breathing plasma fire from his mouth, and Snarl with his tail charged up (EFX).

SNARL: OH WELL…
2 (LINK): … NEVER DID WANT TO LIVE FOREVER!
SLUDGE: **CHAAAARGE!**

Full Script
Here is an example of a page of comic book script. The format which it is written in is known as full script. Here, the writer is very much like the director of a movie, considering each shot and angle and describing what is going on. In this format, the dialogue is included aswell, giving the artist a sense of how much "dead space" he needs to leave for word balloons or captions. The other format used in comic book production is "plot," which describes action over several pages and then the artist decides how the page will take shape. In this case, the dialogue is added after the penciled page is complete.

THUMBNAILS

Before committing to the art board, a wise artist prepares thumbnails of the page first. These quick, loose layouts, normally done at maybe a quarter of the size of the actual page, enable the artist to quickly visualize the page and assess how well it's telling the story. Often, the artist will experiment with different layouts, opting for one or combining elements of two or more.

Layout 1
Here, the artist has allowed for a wide, long shot in the third panel, giving an excellent overview of the whole battle. The raised arm in the final panel overlaps slightly, pushing the character into the foreground.

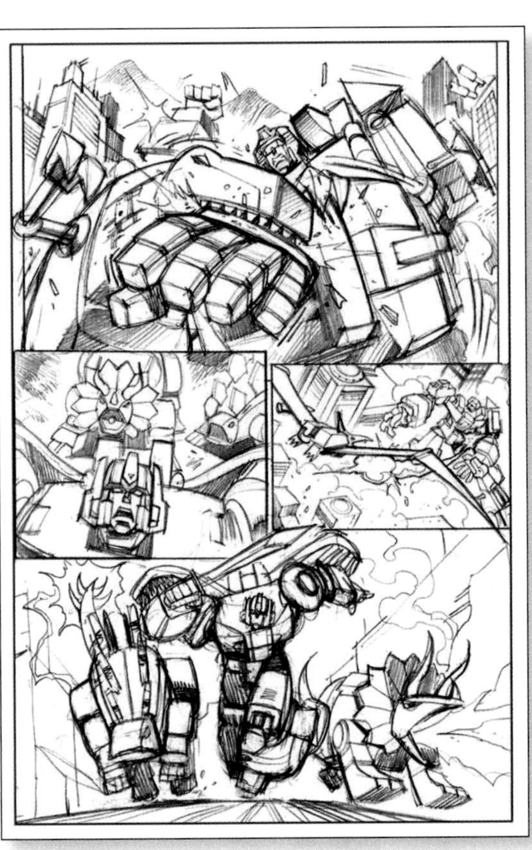

Layout 2
Here, the dramatic up-shot perspective in panel one emphasizes the sheer scale of Devastator, but the impact of panel three is lessened (due to the reduced space).

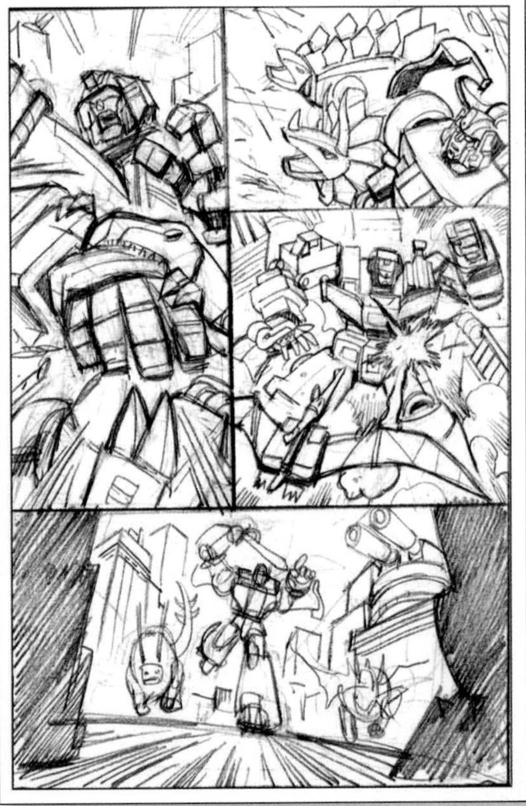

Layout 3
Here, the long thin panel one has a strong vertical feel, while the distance perspective in panel four (with the solid silhouetted legs, extreme foreground) emphasizes that the Dinobots are charging at Devastator.

FINAL LAYOUT

ALL TOGETHER NOW

It's time to bring everything you've learned together on your final page of comic book artwork. Based on the script—you've selected your shots, chosen your layout and made any final decisions on the overall composition. Using your thumbnail as a guide, carefully rule in your panel borders and gutters and lightly sketch in the characters and backgrounds on your art board.

Tightening Up

With the overall layout transferred successfully to the art board, now's the time to start tightening up and finishing your pencil lines. As you can see, the artist has selected layout 1 (from the previous page) and rendered the whole page in finished pencils (including all fine detail and shading). The page is viewed by the editor in case anything needs changing.

SPECIAL EFFECTS

Sound effects (SFX) play an integral part in comic book art. An explosive or concussive impact is enhanced by dramatic, open (for color) lettering, which can be as much artwork as the illustration it complements. Hard metallic sounds, like "KTANNG" and "WHUNK" are particularly prevalent, as the giant robots clash in hand-to-hand combat.

TIPS

Once you have established the layout that will best tell the story, consider the "visual depth" of the whole page. Choose one frame with small and distant figures and one frame with the character filling or even bursting out of the frame. This will add depth and drama to the whole page.
Andrew Wildman

3) Here is the fully inked page. By inserting the speech balloons at pencils stage, the artist has avoided having to ink areas that would have been obscured. The page is now ready for coloring.

3) Here is the fully inked page. By inserting the speech balloons at pencils stage, the artist has avoided having to ink areas that would have been obscured. The page is now ready for coloring.

FINISHED PENCILS
If you look at the script on p88, you'll see that the dialogue was included in the panel descriptions. On viewing the penciled page, the writer will add rough placements, showing where thinks the speech balloons should go:

1) Here, the artist has drawn in the speech balloon borders and tails on the artwork itself, erasing any interior art. This job might also be done by the actual letterer or (on computer) at a later stage.

2) By including the speech balloons at this stage, the artist has made them an integral part of the artwork. Before computers were used, this was standard practice, and some artists still prefer it.

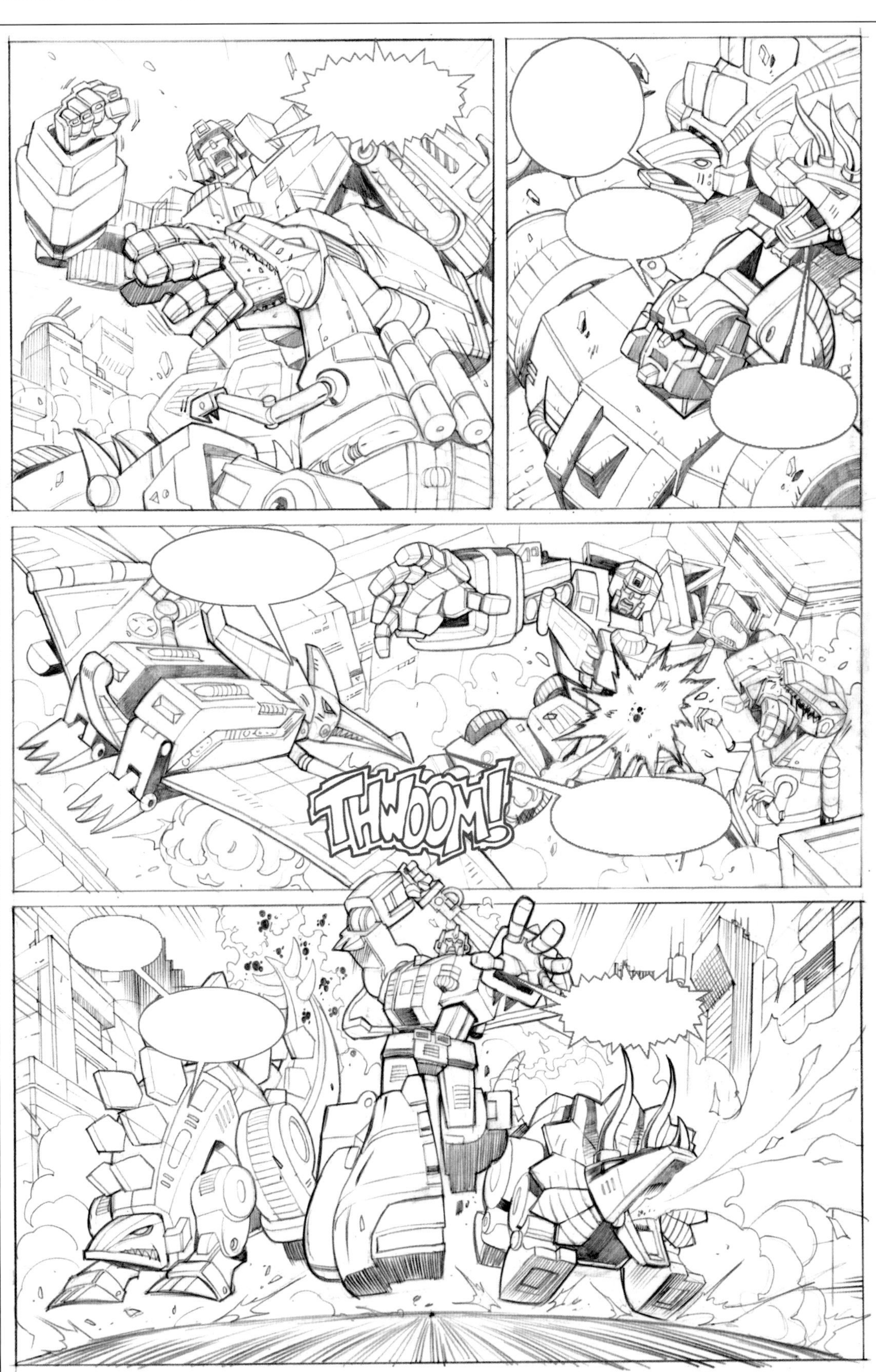

Though, as I've been known to say, "It never ends!"

That's certainly true of TRANSFORMERS itself, a phenomenon that has already lasted more than 20 years and seems—with a live-action movie franchise kicking off in '07—to be showing no signs of slowing down. And just as true of the art and craft of drawing TRANSFORMERS.

My hope is, you've learned much in these pages, certainly enough to get you started on the road to either drawing TRANSFORMERS professionally or just for pleasure. But it's just the beginning. There's so much more to learn, so much of your own style and artistic flair still to emerge and flourish, and the only way that will happen is with practice... and lots of it.

But most of all—enjoy what you do. It's no coincidence that many of the artists currently working professionally in the world of TRANSFORMERS were, first and foremost, fans themselves. Their sheer enthusiasm, and maybe the odd bit of pro instruction along the way, got them to where they are now.

And if they can do it, so can you!

RESOURCES

Books

• The art department of your local library or bookstore will be stocked with a wealth of "how to" books on every aspect of illustration. These will help expand your all-round skills and techniques.

• For a great source of general TRANSFORMERS information, check out Dorling Kindersley's *TRANSFORMERS—The Ultimate Guide*. For character reference, the *TRANSFORMERS: More Than Meets The Eye* guidebooks are must-haves. For hugely insightful interviews with comics creators check out *Artists on Comics Art* (edited by Mark Salisbury), and for great companion volumes to this book, there's *You Can Draw Marvel Characters* by Dan Jurgens and *You Can Draw Star Wars* by Bonnie Burton, both published by Dorling Kindersley.

Websites

• There are a huge number of excellent TRANSFORMERS websites out there, too many to list here. Several have extensive archive sections featuring reviews of the many characters, toys, comics and TV series, and are an excellent resource for the budding TRANSFORMERS artist. Just type "TRANSFORMERS" into a search engine and go.

• The official TRANSFORMERS website can be found at www.hasbro.com

Toys

• One the best sources of (all-angle) artistic reference is, of course, the toys themselves.

INDEX

A

action 34–35
Aerialbots 53
airbrush 37, 79
angle/angle shots 30, 45, 59, 86–87
ankle 46, 47
Ark 38
arm 14–15, 25, 27, 28, 32, 34, 54, 56, 64, 66, 75
Armada 30, 64–65, 68 *see also* Megatron and Minicons
armor 48, 62, 63
Autobot(s) 28, 38, 52–53, 60, 68, 71, 72
  insignia 48
  Matrix of Leadership 58

B

back 34, 63
basic shapes 12–13
  box 58
  circle 12, 13, 34
  combinations of 13
  cube 12, 13, 24
  cuboid 12, 25, 26–27
  curve 18, 30, 69
  cylinder 12, 13, 24, 47, 60
  oval 60
  prism 12
  pyramid 12, 13, 18
  rectangle 12, 19
  sphere 12, 13
  square 12
  triangle 12, 19
battle 36–37
battle damage 48
beard 59
beast wars 60–63 *see also* Maximals and Predacons
beasts 69 *see also* Dinobots and Insecticons
Blaster 87
  female 17
  humanoid 16
  medium guild 16
  oversized 16
  robot 17
Brawn 43
brushes 37, 78, 79
Bumblebee 28

C

chest 15, 28, 34, 38, 39, 56, 63, 64
claws 17, 58, 63
color 37, 79–81, 91 *see also* paint
  digital 37
  effects 82
  properties of 80
  tools for 79
  wheel 82
Combaticons (Bruticus) 57
combiners 56–57
  Constructicons 56
  Devastator 56–57
comic, creating a 84–91
  final layout 90–91
  script 88
  shots and angles 86–87
  special/sound (SFX) effects 90
  speech balloons 91
  storytelling 86
  thumbnails 89, 90
  visualization 88
compasses 11
Cosmos 53
Creation Matrix 38
Cybertron 38, 50, 58, 68–69, 70, 72
Cyber Planet Keys 68–69

D

Decepticons 37, 55, 60, 68, 69, 71, 72 *see also* Insecticons
  insignia 48, 57
  jet 38
  Slag (Triceratops) 55
  Sludge (Brontosaurus) 55
  Snarl (Stegosaurus) 55
  Swoop (Pterandon) 55
Dirt Boss 69
drones 68, 70

E

ears 42, 60
Energon 66–67, 68
  Omnicons 66
  Terrorcons 66
  Tidal Wave 66–67
equipment 10–11, 78
eraser 10
extensions 27
eye level 20, 22
eyebrows 42
eyes 30, 31, 42, 43, 75, 82

F

face 30, 31, 43, 73 *see also* head
figures 14–17
  stick 14, 40, 52, 63
  TRANSFORMER 14
final layout 90–91
finger(s) 11, 44–45, 58
  index 45
fist 34, 44–45
Fizzle 47
foot/toe 15, 17, 25, 26, 33, 35, 44, 46–47, 58, 59, 60
foreshortening 32–33, 40–41, 59, 75
Freeway 47
Frenzy 53

G

Galvatron 47
Generation 1 52, 62, 66
Grapple 66

H

thumb 11, 44–45
head 25, 28, 31, 42–43, 54, 60, 64 *see also* face
Hot Rod 32

I

Inferno 62
inking/inking effects 38, 39, 76–81, 91 *see also* coloring
artwork 37
equipment for 78–79 *see also* brushes; paint and pens
silhouettes 81
textures 80
Insecticons 55
Bombshell 55
Kickback 55
Shrapnel 55
insignia 48, 57
Ironhide 61

J

Jazz 54
Jetfire 53, 68, 69
joints 15, 34, 44, 46–47, 48, 49, 61

K

knee 15, 35, 47

L

leg 14–15, 25, 27, 28, 34–35, 38, 44, 46, 47, 54, 56, 60, 61, 62, 67, 89
light source 30–31, 45, 73 *see also* shading and shadow

M

masterclass: Megatron 72
masterclass: Optimus Prime 38
Maximals 60–61, 63 see also Optimus Primal
Cheetor 61
Rhinox 60
Megatron 30, 33, 34, 62, 63, 65, 72–75, 81
Minicons 64–65
Bonecrusher 65
Dune Runner 65
Grindor 65
Iceberg 65
Ransack 65
Runway 65
Sureshock 65

N

neck 15, 58
nose 42

O

Optimus Primal 60–61
Optimus Prime 22, 34, 38–41, 43, 65, 68, 72, 81, 87

P

paint 79
acrylic, gouache, oil, and watercolor 79
paper 11, 25, 79
pencil drawing 8–75
pencil(s) 10–11, 13, 18, 19, 36, 52, 83, 91
grades of 10
grip 11
pens 37, 78
dip 78
felt-tip/marker 37, 78
technical 78
perspective 20–23, 36, 75, 87 *see also* body perspective
horizon 20, 21
in composition 21
two- and three-point 20
vanishing point 20, 21
planets 68
pose 14, 35, 40, 57, 58, 64, 66, 68
Powerglide 53
Predacons 62–63
Primus, lord of light 58
Prowl 52

R

Rampage 63
Ravage 53
Rhinox 60
Rodimus Prime 66

S

Scattershot 69
Scorponok 17, 62
script and thumbnails *see* comic, creating a
shading 30–31, 36, 37, 38, 40, 60, 75, 90 *see also* light source
highlights/lowlights 30
mood 30
shadow 30, 31, 45, 73, 75
Shockwave 43
shoulder 15, 40, 64
Sideswipe 17
Silverbolt (eagle) 61
skin 60, 61
stick figure 14, 40, 52, 63
Stormbringer 70–71, 80
Bludgeon 69
centurion drones 70
Thunderwing 69, 70
Stunticons (Menasor) 57

T

Tarantulas 62, 63
texture 37, 80
Thunderwing 68, 69, 80
torso 14–15, 25, 40, 56, 62
transforming characters 24–29
extensions 27
foldout limbs 27
Frenzy: Decepticon mini-cassette/robot 25
and full transformation 28–29
twists/turns 26
triangle/set square 11

U

Ultra Magnus 66
Unicron 58–59

V

vehicles 18–19, 28, 37, 67, 69
aircraft carrier 67
Starscream 19, 43, 53
Sunstreaker 18
Velocitron (speed planet) 69
vents 48

W

Waspinator 62, 63
weapons 28, 38, 50–51, 70, 74
Wheeljack 4
wheels and tracks 48
wings 19, 58, 59, 63
wrist 11, 74

ACKNOWLEDGMENTS

AUTHOR ACKNOWLEDGMENTS

First and foremost, I'd like to thank Guido Guidi for his excellent step-by-step illustrations for the book. Their quality and clarity made my job that much easier. I'd also like to thank all the other artists who kindly gave of their time (and know-how) to provide the "TIPS" scattered throughout. Thanks also to Chris Ryall and Dan Taylor at IDW Publishing and Dan Jurgens (who provided the template for the *You Can Draw* series). And, last but not least, the legions of fans who continue to loyally support TRANSFORMERS in all its incarnations and media.

PUBLISHER'S ACKNOWLEDGMENTS

DK would like to thank Michael Kelly, Ed Lane, and Frances Hinds at Hasbro for their assistance; Marian Anderson for the indexing; and Guidi Guido, Marcelo Matere, Nick Roche, E.J. Su, and Andrew Wildman for their tips.